# Girl Food

## Other Books by Cathy Guisewite

Understanding the "Why" Chromosome

The Child Within Has Been Awakened But the Old Lady on the
    Outside Just Collapsed

Revelations from a 45-Pound Purse

Only Love Can Break a Heart, But a Shoe Sale Can Come Close

$14 in the Bank and a $200 Face in My Purse

My Granddaughter Has Fleas!!

Why Do the Right Words Always Come Out of the Wrong Mouth?

A Hand to Hold, an Opinion to Reject

Thin Thighs in Thirty Years

Wake Me Up When I'm a Size 5

Men Should Come with Instruction Booklets

A Mouthful of Breath Mints and No One to Kiss

Another Saturday Night of Wild and Reckless Abandon

Reflections: A Fifteenth Anniversary Collection

Cathy Twentieth Anniversary Collection

## Other Books by Barbara Albright

Entertaining with Regis & Kathie Lee

Cooking with Regis & Kathie Lee

Quick Chocolate Fixes (with Leslie Weiner)

Totally Teabreads (with Leslie Weiner)

Completely Cookies (with Leslie Weiner)

Simply Scones (with Leslie Weiner)

Wild About Brownies (with Leslie Weiner)

Mostly Muffins (with Leslie Weiner)

# Girl Food

*Cathy's Cookbook for the Well-Balanced Woman*

Cathy Guisewite
*and*
Barbara Albright

**Andrews McMeel
Publishing**

Kansas City

Designed by Randall Blair Design.

Library of Congress Cataloging-in-Publication Data
Guisewite, Cathy.
    Girl food : cathy's cookbook for the well-balanced woman / Cathy Guisewite and Barbara Albright.
            p.    cm.
    Includes index.
    ISBN 0-8362-3173-2 (hardcover)
    1. Cookery.   2. Women—Humor.   I. Albright, Barbara.  II. Title.
TX714.G85    1997
641.5--dc20                                                          96-44336
                                                                       CIP

First Printing, June 1997

Second Printing, October 1997

# Contents

# Introduction

This is the cookbook that speaks to women.
Women who want romance.
Women who require chocolate.
Women who dream of wearing a swimsuit somewhere
besides the bathroom.
Women who need to entertain like a sophisticated grown-up.
Women who want to lie on the sofa in a sweat suit and eat
cookie dough.
In short, women whose lives are a little too complex to have
only one sort of recipe on hand at any given moment.

Here in one book, each woman will find a voice.
Each woman within each woman will find a recipe.
And every one of us can raise a fork, triumphant in the
knowledge that even if the world doesn't quite understand us,
at least there's a cookbook that does.

# Romance Food

# Romance Food

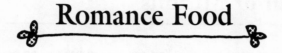

I once spent $218.74 preparing a romantic chicken dinner for a man: $120 in phone calls to girlfriends asking what I should make, $30 in phone calls to my mother asking how to make it, $50 to my therapist asking why I was making it, $12 for the pan, and $6.74 for the chicken.

What will work? That's all we really want to know, isn't it?

What will catapult me from "dinner companion" to "Irresistible Goddess" the fastest?

What will make him instantly oblivious to a few excess pounds, a few extra wrinkles, and/or the fact that prior to this evening, I didn't actually know how to cook anything that didn't have microwave instructions written on the side?

What will lure him away from the NFL, NHL, NBA, PGA, and the World Wide Web?

And most important, what will I do to sustain the fantasy if meal number one works as planned and he can't wait to taste what I have in mind for meal number two?

## *After Commiserating with Twelve of My Closest Girlfriends, We've Decided He Really Loves Me* Apricot Walnut Muffins

**These muffins go together very quickly. You can also substitute an equal quantity of other "mix-ins" (such as chocolate chips, other dried fruits, and nuts) for the apricots and walnuts.**

**2 cups all-purpose flour**

**1/2 cup firmly packed brown sugar**

**2 teaspoons baking powder**

**1/4 teaspoon salt**

**3/4 cup milk**

**1/2 cup (1 stick) unsalted butter, melted and cooled**

**1 large egg, lightly beaten**

**2 teaspoons vanilla extract**

**1 cup chopped walnuts**

**1 cup chopped dried apricots**

Preheat the oven to 400°F. Butter or lightly coat with non-stick vegetable cooking spray twelve 3-by-1 1/4-inch (3 1/2- to 4-ounce) muffin cups.

In a large bowl, stir together the flour, brown sugar, baking powder, and salt. In another bowl, stir together the milk, butter, egg, and vanilla until blended. Make a well in the center of the dry ingredients. Add the milk mixture and stir just to blend. Stir in the walnuts and apricots to combine.

Spoon the batter evenly among the prepared muffin cups. Bake for 15 to 20 minutes, or until a cake tester inserted into the center of one muffin comes out clean and the muffins are just starting to brown.

Remove the muffin tin or tins to a wire rack. Cool for 5 minutes before removing the muffins from the cups; finish cooling on the rack. Serve warm or cool completely and store in an airtight container at room temperature.

Makes 12 muffins.

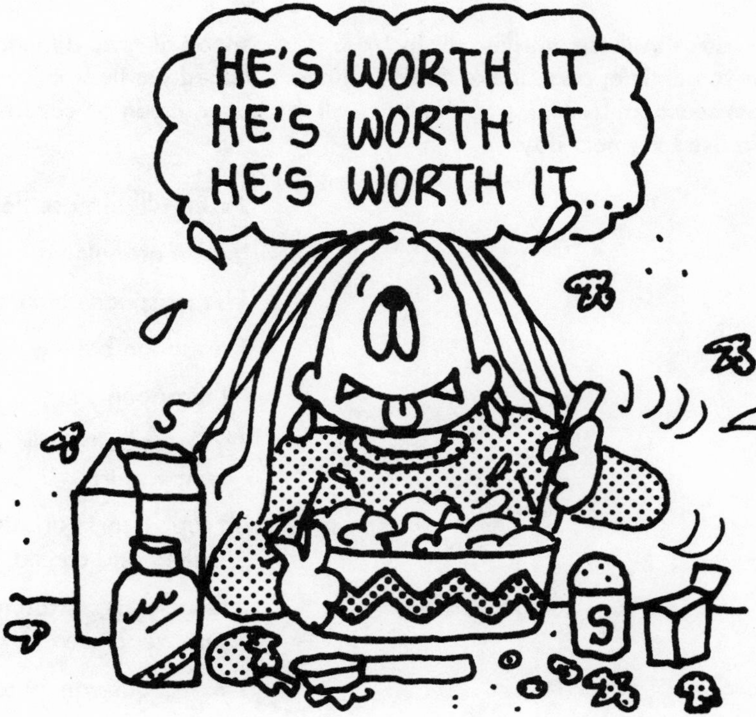
HE'S WORTH IT
HE'S WORTH IT
HE'S WORTH IT...

## *While He Casually Reads the Morning Paper, I'll Be Silently Planning Out the Course of Our Entire Relationship* **Waffles**

To add a hint of citrus to these waffles, stir in 1/4 to 1/2 teaspoon of grated fresh orange or lemon zest.  For romantic appeal, make these in a heart-shaped waffle iron.  Serve with a salad made from seasonal fruits. If you don't use all the batter, it can be covered and refrigerated and used the next day.

2 cups all-purpose flour

1/3 cup granulated sugar

1 1/2 teaspoons baking powder

1 teaspoon baking soda

1/4 teaspoon salt

1 1/2 cups buttermilk, at room temperature

1/2 cup (1 stick) unsalted butter, melted and cooled

2 large eggs, at room temperature, separated

2 teaspoons vanilla extract

Preheat the waffle iron according to the manufacturer's instructions. (The iron is ready when a few drops of water sprinkled onto the surface immediately turn into dancing droplets.)

In a large bowl, stir together the flour, sugar, baking powder, baking soda, and salt. In another bowl, stir together the buttermilk, butter, egg yolks, and vanilla. Make a well in the center of the flour mixture. Add the liquid ingredients and stir just to combine.

In a grease-free medium bowl, using a handheld electric mixer set at medium-high speed, beat the egg whites until they just start to form stiff peaks when the beaters are lifted.

Using a rubber spatula, fold one third of the beaten egg whites into the batter to lighten it. Fold in the remaining egg whites.

Pour the mixture into the center of the preheated waffle iron, filling it about two-thirds full. Cook the waffles for 3 to 5 minutes, or until they are set (steam will stop coming out from the edges). Transfer the waffles to a warm oven and continue making the waffles until all the batter is used. Serve immediately.

Makes about 8 waffles.

## *The Less Time I Spend Making Breakfast, the More Time I Can Spend on My Makeup*
## Quick Crumb-Topped Banana Coffee Cake

Here's an easy cake that will use up ripe bananas. If you have bananas that are ripe, but don't have time to cook with them right away, peel and store them in an airtight container in the freezer for up to three months. Let them thaw before mashing and using in recipes.

*Crumb Topping:*

1/2 cup all-purpose flour

1/4 cup firmly packed brown sugar

1/4 teaspoon ground cinnamon

1/4 cup (1/2 stick) unsalted butter, chilled and cut into 1/2-inch cubes

*Banana Cake:*

2 cups all-purpose flour

1 1/2 teaspoons baking powder

1/2 teaspoon baking soda

1/2 teaspoon salt

1 cup mashed ripe bananas (about 2 medium bananas)

1/3 cup milk, at room temperature

2 teaspoons vanilla extract

1/2 cup (1 stick) unsalted butter, at room temperature

1 cup granulated sugar

2 large eggs, at room temperature

Preheat the oven to 350°F. Butter a 9-inch square or round baking pan.

*To make the crumb topping:*
In a medium bowl, stir together the flour, brown sugar, and cinnamon. Add the butter cubes. Using your fingertips, quickly rub the butter into the flour mixture until the mixture resembles small peas. Set aside.

*To make the banana cake:*
In a medium bowl, stir together the flour, baking powder, baking soda, and salt. In another medium bowl, stir together the bananas, milk, and vanilla. In a large bowl, using a hand-held electric mixer, cream together the butter and sugar until blended. One at a time, add the eggs, beating well after each addition. In three additions each, alternately beat in the flour mixture and the banana mixture, just until combined.

Scrape the batter into the prepared pan, smoothing the surface with a spatula. Sprinkle the top evenly with the crumb topping. Bake for 40 to 45 minutes, or until a cake tester or tooth-pick inserted into the center of the cake comes out clean and the cake is lightly browned.

Transfer the cake to a wire rack and cool. Serve warm.

Makes 9 servings.

# *Instead of Using the Old Saran Wrap and Stiletto Heels Approach to Spice Things Up, I Think I'll Try Some Aphrodisiac* Asparagus Vinaigrette

Asparagus is purported to have aphrodisiacal properties. In fact, in nineteenth-century France the bridegroom's prenuptial dinner was supposed to contain three courses of asparagus! Served on a bed of lettuce, this salad first course can be made ahead of time to provide an elegant beginning to any meal. As far as asparagus's seductive powers, it's worth a try!

**1 bunch of asparagus (about 1 1/4 pounds when purchased)**

**1/2 cup water**

**1/2 teaspoon salt**

**1 cup of Basic Vinaigrette (recipe follows)**

**Lettuce leaves (optional)**

Hold each stalk of asparagus and bend to snap off the tough base portion. If the asparagus are especially tough, peel the stalks with a vegetable peeler. Wash the asparagus in water, rinsing well so that no grit remains.

In a large skillet, bring the water and salt to a boil. Add the asparagus, cover, and simmer for 6 to 8 minutes, or until the asparagus are crisp-tender. Drain the asparagus well and place them in a large shallow bowl. Add the Basic Vinaigrette, cover, and refrigerate for up to 24 hours, tossing occasionally to coat with the vinaigrette. Serve on a bed of lettuce, if desired.

Makes 4 servings.

# Basic Romance Vinaigrette

Classic vinaigrette recipes use a ratio of three parts oil to one part vinegar. In this recipe we've used less oil, resulting in a tangier vinaigrette. If it is too tangy for your liking, increase the oil. Decrease the oil if you want it to be tangier. This basic recipe also lends itself to many variations. If you have fresh herbs, chop them up and add them to the dressing. In addition to being perfect for tossing with fresh salad ingredients (buy the pre-cut packaged variety if you are in a hurry), vinaigrette is also delicious as a marinade for grilled or broiled meat, chicken, fish, or vegetables.

3/4 cup vegetable oil

1/4 cup olive oil

2/3 cup red wine vinegar

1 tablespoon Dijon-style mustard

1 tablespoon freshly squeezed lemon juice

1 teaspoon dried basil leaves, crushed

1 medium garlic clove, cut in half

1/4 teaspoon dried oregano leaves, crushed

1/4 teaspoon dried thyme leaves, crushed

1/2 teaspoon salt

Dash of freshly ground pepper

Dash of Tabasco pepper sauce

In a large screw-top jar or a small bowl, shake or whisk together all of the ingredients. Remove the garlic halves before using the dressing. Refrigerate leftover dressing.

Makes about 2 cups dressing.

# *He Actually Believed Me When I Said I Could Cook* Seduction Steak with Portobello Mushroom Sauce

When it comes to appealing to a man, sometimes it pays to go for the beef. Let him do the manly grilling and you take care of the sauce. Just like the two of you, this steak is a perfect partner with Parmesan Sun-Dried Tomato Potatoes (page 21).

**Portobello Mushroom Sauce:**

**1 tablespoon butter**

**1/2 pound sliced portobello mushrooms**

**1/4 cup chopped shallots**

**1/4 teaspoon salt**

**Dash of freshly ground black pepper**

**1 cup beef stock or broth**

**1/4 cup dry red wine**

**Steaks:**

**2 tender steaks (such as T-bone, porterhouse, or sirloin), each cut about 1 1/2 inches thick**

**Salt and pepper to taste**

*To make the portobello mushroom sauce:*
In a medium skillet, melt the butter over medium heat. Add the mushrooms, shallots, salt, and pepper. Cook for about 5 minutes, stirring occasionally. Add the broth and wine. Increase the heat to high and continue cooking until the mixture has been reduced by half.

*To make the steaks:*
Preheat the grill or broiler. Position the grill or broiler rack approximately 4 inches from the heat source. Grill or broil the steaks for 4 to 10 minutes on each side depending on the desired degree of doneness. Season with salt and pepper. Serve with the portobello mushroom sauce.

Makes 2 servings.

## *Cupid Is Alive and Well and Living in My Kitchen*
# Cornish Hens

**This recipe is for two Cornish hens. If love leaves, simply cut this recipe in half for a singular, forlorn lovebird.**

**2 Cornish hens (about 1 1/4 pounds each)**

**1/2 teaspoon salt**

**1 tablespoon melted butter, divided**

**3 tablespoons apricot preserves**

**1 tablespoon Dijon-style mustard**

**Fruit and Nut Pilaf (page 18)**

Preheat the oven to 400°F. Wash and pat dry hens. Sprinkle the inside of each hen with 1/4 teaspoon of the salt. Place the hens, breast side up, on a rack set in a shallow roasting or baking pan. Brush the hens with half of the butter. Roast for 15 minutes. Brush the hens with the remaining half of the butter. Roast for 15 minutes longer.

Meanwhile, in a small saucepan, melt the apricot preserves over low heat. Stir in the mustard to combine and remove the pan from the heat. Brush the hens with the glaze and roast about 15 minutes longer, or until the hens are golden brown and the juices run clear when the hens are pierced with a fork. Serve with Fruit and Nut Pilaf.

Makes 2 servings.

## *Love Means Never Having to Say, "Of Course I Like Football"* Pork Tenderloin

This tenderloin is seasoned with an Asian-style marinade. The leftover marinade is cooked to form a delicious sauce. Serve it with rice and some steamed crisp-tender vegetables.

3 tablespoons tamari sauce (see Note)

1 tablespoon oriental-style sesame oil

1 tablespoon Dijon-style mustard

1 tablespoon finely chopped gingerroot

1 scallion, finely chopped (including the tender green tops)

1 medium garlic clove, finely chopped

1/8 teaspoon Tabasco pepper sauce

1 whole pork tenderloin (about 1 pound)

1/2 cup chicken broth

1 teaspoon cornstarch

In a large bowl, stir together the tamari, sesame oil, mustard, gingerroot, scallion, garlic, and pepper sauce. Add the pork tenderloin and turn to coat with the marinade mixture. Refrigerate for at least 2 hours, turning the tenderloin occasionally.

Preheat the grill or broiler. Position the grill or broiler rack approximately 6 inches from the heat source. Place the tenderloin on the grill or broiling pan. Grill or broil the tenderloin for about 10 minutes, turn and grill the other side for 10 minutes more, or until the tenderloin is completely cooked through. (It will register 160°F. on a meat thermometer.)

Meanwhile, add the remaining marinade mixture to a small saucepan. Stir the broth and cornstarch together to combine and add this to the marinade mixture. Cook over high heat and let the mixture boil for 1 minute, stirring constantly, until the sauce has thickened slightly. Slice the cooked tenderloin and serve with the sauce.

Makes 2 to 3 servings.

Note: *Tamari sauce is a traditional Japanese soy seasoning available in the Asian section of grocery stores.*

# *If the Way to His Heart Is Through His Stomach, This Will Be a Direct Hit* Fruit and Nut Pilaf

**2 teaspoons butter, divided**

**¹/4 cup chopped onion**

**¹/2 cup uncooked long-grain white rice**

**1 cup chicken broth**

**Salt to taste**

**¹/8 teaspoon freshly ground pepper**

**¹/4 cup pine nuts**

**¹/4 cup chopped dried apricots**

In a medium saucepan, melt 1 teaspoon of the butter over medium heat.  Add the onion and cook for about 5 minutes, or until softened.  Add the rice and cook, stirring constantly, for 2 to 3 minutes, or until opaque.  Add the chicken broth, salt, and pepper.  Increase the heat to high and bring the mixture to a boil, stirring occasionally.  Cover the pan, reduce the heat to low, and simmer for 18 to 20 minutes, or until the rice has absorbed all the liquid.

In another small saucepan, melt the remaining teaspoon of butter over medium heat.  Add the pine nuts and cook for 2 minutes, or until the nuts are lightly browned.  Stir the nuts and apricots into the rice mixture.  Heat through.

Makes 2 to 3 servings.

# *This Will Make Him Forget He Ever Saw Me on a Bad Hair Day* Pasta Puttanesca

This classic Italian pasta sauce is named after the *puttane* — the Italian ladies of the night. Its bold and lusty flavor is sure to make this a favorite in your kitchen when you want good eating. Serve it with an equally bold red wine, a tossed green salad, and a crusty loaf of bread to complete this feast.

6 ounces linguine or spaghetti

2 teaspoons olive oil

1 medium garlic clove, finely chopped

1 can (28 ounces) plum tomatoes, drained and chopped

1/4 cup black olives, sliced and pitted

1 tablespoon capers, drained

2 anchovy fillets, drained and mashed

1/2 teaspoon dried basil leaves, crushed

1/8 teaspoon dried oregano leaves, crushed

Pinch of crushed red pepper flakes

Salt and freshly ground pepper to taste

Chopped Italian flat or curly leaf parsley (optional)

Grated Parmesan or Romano cheese (optional)

Cook the pasta according to the package directions and drain.

Meanwhile, in a large skillet, heat the oil over medium heat. Add the garlic and cook for about 1 minute, or until the garlic has softened slightly. Add the drained tomatoes, olives, capers, anchovies, basil, oregano, and crushed red pepper flakes. Bring the mixture to a boil, stirring occasionally. Reduce the heat and simmer for about 15 minutes. Season with salt and pepper. Serve over the cooked pasta. Sprinkle with parsley and grated cheese, if desired.

Makes 2 generous servings.

# AACK! *He Found My Yearbook*
## Salmon Potato Don't Fret Frittata

Delicious for breakfast, lunch, or dinner — or even for a very early morning breakfast after the party — a frittata is an Italian omelet that is cooked on both sides.  Use this recipe as a basic frittata for creating your own varieties.

**1 tablespoon olive oil**

**1 tablespoon butter**

**1 medium red potato, scrubbed and cut into ¹/₂-inch cubes**

**1 scallion, finely chopped (including tender green tops)**

**4 large eggs**

**2 ounces smoked salmon (lox), cut into slivers**

**Salt and freshly ground pepper to taste**

In an 8-inch skillet, heat the oil and butter over medium heat.  Add the potato cubes and cook, stirring occasionally, for 15 to 20 minutes, or until the potatoes are tender.  Add the scallion and cook 1 minute longer.  If your skillet does not have an ovenproof handle, wrap it with a double thickness of aluminum foil to protect it.

Meanwhile, in a medium bowl, whisk together the eggs, salmon, salt, and pepper just until combined.  Position the broiler rack so it is about 6 inches from the heat source.  Preheat the broiler.

Add the egg mixture to the skillet with the potato mixture.  Stir slightly just until it begins to set.  Then place the skillet under the broiler for 1 to 2 minutes, or until the egg mixture puffs and starts to brown lightly.  Cut the frittata into wedges to serve.

Makes 2 servings.

## *Extremely Passionate*
# Parmesan Sun-Dried Tomato Potatoes

These flavorful twice-baked potatoes are filled with a delicious mixture that includes Parmesan cheese, sun-dried tomatoes, and scallions. Heat the milk in your microwave oven in a microwave-safe measuring cup. While you are preparing these, stuff more potatoes to enjoy another day. Cover and refrigerate the additional potatoes until you are ready to reheat them in the microwave oven.

**2 large Idaho potatoes**

**1/3 to 1/2 cup hot milk**

**2 tablespoons butter, softened**

**1/2 teaspoon salt**

**Pinch of freshly ground pepper**

**2 tablespoons oil-packed sun-dried tomatoes, drained and chopped**

**2 tablespoons scallions, finely chopped (including tender green tops)**

**1 tablespoon grated Parmesan cheese**

Preheat the oven to 425°F. Scrub the potatoes well and then pierce them almost to the center with the tines of a fork (this will allow steam to escape and it will keep the potatoes from bursting during baking). Place the potatoes directly on the oven rack and bake for about 1 hour, or until tender. Remove the potatoes from the oven and position the rack about 5 inches away from the heat source. Preheat the broiler.

Cut a 1/4-inch-thick lengthwise slice off the top of each potato. Using a metal spoon, carefully scoop the insides of the potatoes into a medium bowl. Add 1/3 cup of the milk, butter, salt, and pepper. Using a handheld electric mixer, beat the potato mixture until smooth, adding additional hot milk if necessary to create a smooth mixture. Add the tomatoes, scallions, and Parmesan cheese and beat just until combined.

Spoon the mixture into the potato shells. Place the potatoes on a broiler pan and broil for 1 to 2 minutes, or until the tops are lightly browned.

Makes 2 servings.

# *Even Though He's Sound Asleep on the Couch, I Know He'll Protect Me* **Hero Sandwich**

This hearty man-sized sandwich is layered with cheese and meat and then smothered with a flavorful cooked vegetable mixture. It is a perfect sandwich for a picnic or tailgate party.

2 tablespoons olive oil

1 small onion, thinly sliced

1 garlic clove, finely chopped

1 small eggplant, thinly sliced

1 medium zucchini, thinly sliced

1 small tomato, thinly sliced

1/2 red or green bell pepper, seeded and thinly sliced

1/2 cup sliced mushrooms

2 tablespoons red wine vinegar

1/2 teaspoon dried basil leaves, crushed

1/4 teaspoon dried oregano leaves, crushed

1/4 teaspoon salt

Dash of freshly ground pepper

1 loaf Italian or French bread (about 8 ounces)

3/4 pound total of your favorite thinly sliced luncheon meats and cheeses (such as salami, provolone, Muenster, Swiss, Cheddar, ham, smoked or regular turkey)

2 tablespoons grated Parmesan cheese

In a large skillet, heat the oil over medium-high heat. Add the onion and garlic and cook for about 5 minutes, or until softened slightly. Add the eggplant, zucchini, tomato, pepper, mushrooms, vinegar, basil, oregano, salt, and pepper. Simmer for 15 to 20 minutes, or until the vegetables are softened and most of the liquid has evaporated, stirring the mixture occasionally. Remove the pan from the heat and cool.

Slice the loaf of bread in half lengthwise and scoop out most of the soft insides. Line both sides of the loaf with the meats and cheeses. Evenly distribute the vegetables over the meats and cheeses. Sprinkle the surface with the Parmesan cheese. Place the halves of the sandwich together. Wrap in foil or plastic wrap. Unwrap the loaf and use a serrated knife to cut the sandwich into slices.

Makes 2 very generous servings.

## *Would You Like to Stop by the Jewelry Store on the Way to the Hockey Game* Chocolate Chip Brownies

Chocolate speaks the language of love. These dense rich brownies are speckled with chocolate chips. They are perfect for picnics, and to mail to him when he's out of town. You can also use a square of these brownies as the base for a brownie sundae. Top it with a scoop of ice cream, drizzle with Hot Fudge Sauce (page 123), and add a dollop of sweetened whipped cream.

1 cup (2 sticks) unsalted butter

4 ounces unsweetened chocolate, broken into pieces

3 ounces bittersweet chocolate, broken into pieces

4 large eggs, at room temperature

1 cup granulated sugar

1/2 cup firmly packed brown sugar

1 tablespoon vanilla extract

1 cup all-purpose flour

1/4 teaspoon salt

1 1/2 cups semisweet chocolate chips

1 cup chopped walnuts or pecans (optional)

Preheat the oven to 350°F. Line a 13-by-9-inch baking pan with aluminum foil so that the foil extends 2 inches beyond the two long sides of the pan. Lightly butter the bottom and sides of the foil-lined pan.

In a large microwave-safe bowl, heat the butter and chocolates in a microwave oven on high for 1 to 3 minutes, stirring halfway through cooking, until the chocolate is melted (or use a double boiler over hot, not simmering, water). Let it stand at room temperature for 20 minutes.

In a large bowl, using a handheld electric mixer set at medium-high speed, beat the eggs and sugars for 2 to 3 minutes, or until the mixture is light in color. Beat in the chocolate mixture and vanilla until blended. Beat in the flour and salt just until combined. Using a wooden spoon, stir in the chocolate chips and the nuts, if desired.

Scrape the batter into the prepared pan and spread evenly. Bake for 30 to 40 minutes, or until a toothpick inserted into the center comes out with fudgy crumbs. Cool the brownies in the pan set on a wire rack. Cut into rectangles.

These brownies freeze well.

Makes 20 brownies.

## *After Five Hundred and Two Dinners and Four Hundred and Twenty-Seven Cups of Coffee, I Think It's Time to Get Serious* Marry Me Mousse

This decadent mousse uses raspberry-flavored liqueur.  Serve it in stemmed dessert glasses or wineglasses and garnish each serving with a few raspberries and a sprig of mint or a dollop of sweetened whipped cream and a few chocolate curls.  Try the recipe with other flavors of liqueur such as orange-flavored liqueur or cognac.

9 ounces bittersweet chocolate, broken into pieces

1/2 cup milk

A few grains of salt

1 tablespoon vegetable oil

1 tablespoon black raspberry liqueur (such as Chambord)

1 1/2 teaspoons vanilla extract

1 cup heavy (whipping) cream, chilled

In the container of a food processor fitted with a metal chopping blade, process the chocolate for 20 to 30 seconds, or until it is finely chopped.

In a small saucepan, over medium heat, cook the milk and salt, until the mixture just comes to a boil, stirring occasionally with a wooden spoon. Remove the pan from the heat.

With the motor of the food processor running, pour the hot milk through the feed tube. Process for 10 to 20 seconds, or until the chocolate is completely melted. Add the oil, liqueur, and vanilla and process for 5 to 10 seconds longer, or until the mixture is combined. Scrape the mixture into a large bowl and let stand for 20 to 30 minutes, or until cool.

In a chilled large bowl, using a handheld electric mixer with chilled beaters, beat the cream until peaks just start to form.

Using a rubber spatula, gently fold one third of the whipped cream into the chocolate mixture to lighten it. Fold in the remaining whipped cream just until combined.

Spoon the mixture into four stemmed dessert glasses or wineglasses. Cover the glasses with plastic wrap and refrigerate for 1 to 2 hours, or until the mixture is set. The mousse may be prepared up to 2 days in advance.

Makes 4 servings.

## *He'll Keep Coming Back for More*
# Amore Amaretto Cheesecake

Cream-filled chocolate sandwich cookies form the easy crust for this decadent chocolate-swirled cheesecake. If you have a food processor, process the cookies using a metal chopping blade until they are crushed. Add the melted butter and process about 30 seconds longer or until the mixture is combined.

*Cookie Crust:*

16 cream-filled chocolate sandwich cookies (such as Oreos), crushed into crumbs

2 tablespoons unsalted butter, melted

*Chocolate-Swirled Amaretto Cheesecake Filling:*

2 packages (8 ounces each) cream cheese, softened

1 cup granulated sugar

1 tablespoon all-purpose flour

3 large eggs, at room temperature

1/2 cup sour cream, at room temperature

1/4 cup amaretto

1 teaspoon vanilla extract

2 ounces semisweet chocolate, melted and cooled

*To make the cookie crust:*
Preheat the oven to 325°F. Lightly butter the bottom and side of an 8-inch springform pan. Place the pan on a piece of aluminum foil and press it to cover the bottom and part of the side to prevent any batter from leaking out.

In a medium bowl, stir together the crushed cookies and the butter. Using your fingertips, press the mixture firmly and evenly onto the bottom and 3/4 inch up the side of the prepared pan.

*To make the filling:*
In a large bowl, using a handheld electric mixer, beat the cream cheese just until smooth. Beat in the sugar and flour. Beat in the eggs one at a time. Using a wooden spoon, stir in the sour cream, amaretto, and vanilla.

Scrape all but 3 tablespoons of the batter into the prepared pan. In a small bowl, stir together the reserved batter and the melted chocolate until combined.

Pour the chocolate in 1/2-inch-wide parallel lines, about 1 inch apart, on top of the filling. Insert the tip of a small knife about 1/2 inch deep into the filling. Working perpendicular to the chocolate strips, draw the knife back and forth in lines to create a feathery marbled effect.

Bake for 45 to 55 minutes, or until the center of the cheesecake is set and it is just beginning to brown around the edge. Turn off the oven and open the door slightly. Let the cheesecake stand in the oven for 30 minutes longer. Remove the cake to a wire rack and cool completely.

Cover the top of the springform pan tightly with plastic wrap and refrigerate overnight, or for at least 4 hours, until well chilled. Take the cheesecake from the refrigerator 30 minutes before serving and remove the side of the springform pan. Cut the cheesecake into wedges with a sharp, thin knife.

Makes about 10 servings.

# Swimsuit Food

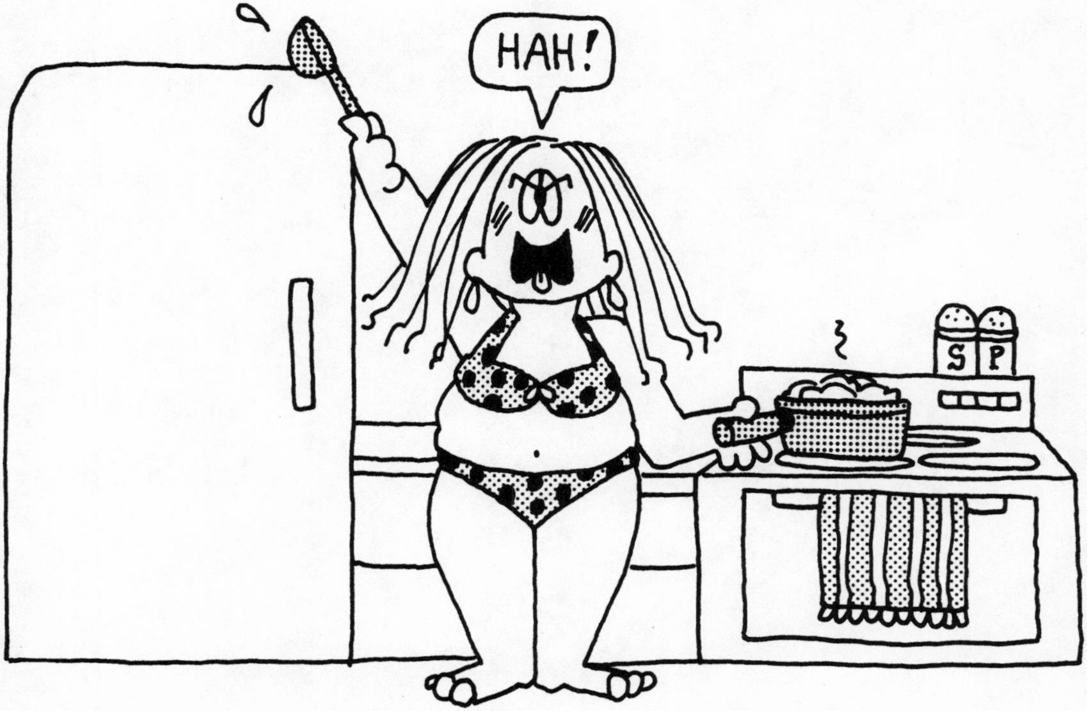
HAH!
S
P

# Swimsuit Food

Nothing compels me toward "sensible eating" like getting a good look at my winter body in a summer mirror. Okay, fine, maybe I should have taken a peek before June 1. Perhaps it was a mistake to wear baggy long skirts with elastic waistbands for the past six months. Possibly the swimwear manufacturers aren't entirely to blame.

Still, I feel I've suffered enough just by walking into the swimwear department. I shouldn't also have to deprive myself of food.

Besides, the body is in natural harmony with the changing of the seasons and since mid-March has been belligerently rejecting anything that hints of "low fat."

It's not just time for action. It's time for trickery. Fool the fat cells into thinking they're getting a nice, big breakfast. Fool the stomach into thinking it's had a full-calorie lunch. Fool the thighs into believing they're getting chocolate cake.

Look this fat-free, reduced-calorie, lite, boring world in the eye, say "HAH!" and then march into the kitchen and make something that's guiltless *and* good to eat.

And for once make the words "active lifestyle" mean something besides standing in the swimwear dressing room ripping a ten-inch piece of floral spandex to shreds.

## *It's Monday and I'm Motivated*
## Low-Fat Bran Muffins

Here's a muffin recipe with a minimum amount of fat. Its moist texture is a result of using plain yogurt and applesauce.

2 cups bran cereal
(such as All-Bran)

1 cup plain low-fat yogurt

²/₃ cup chunky applesauce

¹/₂ cup skim milk

1¹/₂ cups all-purpose flour

1 teaspoon ground cinnamon

1 teaspoon baking powder

1 teaspoon baking soda

¹/₄ teaspoon salt

2 large eggs

2 tablespoons molasses

1 tablespoon vegetable oil

1 teaspoon vanilla extract

¹/₃ cup firmly packed brown
sugar

Preheat the oven to 400°F. Butter or lightly coat with nonstick vegetable cooking spray twelve 3-by-1 1/4-inch (3 1/2- to 4-ounce) muffin cups.

In a large bowl stir together the cereal, yogurt, applesauce, and skim milk. Let the mixture stand until the liquid is absorbed. Meanwhile assemble the remaining ingredients.

In a large bowl, stir together the flour, cinnamon, baking powder, baking soda, and salt.

In another large bowl, stir together the eggs, molasses, oil, and vanilla until combined. Stir in the brown sugar. Stir in the bran mixture until combined. Make a well in the center of the flour mixture and stir in the egg-bran mixture just to combine.

Spoon the batter evenly among the prepared muffin cups. Bake for 15 to 20 minutes, or until a cake tester inserted into the center of one muffin comes out clean.

Remove the muffin tin or tins to a wire rack. Cool for 5 minutes before removing the muffins from the cups; finish cooling on the rack. Serve warm or cool completely and store in an airtight container at cool room temperature.

These muffins freeze well.

Makes 12 muffins.

## *I Don't Want to Go Shopping; I Have to Eat Healthy; What's in the Fridge* Vegetable Omelet for One

One of the easiest and most satisfying meals is an omelet. A plain omelet is terrific on its own, but often your refrigerator holds the makings for some delicious fillings or toppings, either savory or sweet. A vegetable filling has fewer calories than one that includes cheese. A hot-cheese omelet, however, could provide a feeling of satisifaction and keep you from snacking later on. Because the actual omelet cooks very quickly, prepare the filling before you are ready to fill the omelet. To keep the eggs hot when you serve them, run your plate under hot water to take off the chill and dry it before you top it with your freshly cooked hot omelet.

### Basic Omelet:

**2 large eggs**

**2 tablespoons water**

**1/8 teaspoon salt**

**Dash of freshly ground pepper**

**2 teaspoons unsalted butter**

In a small bowl, whisk together the eggs, water, salt, and pepper until blended.

In a 7- to 10-inch nonstick skillet, cook the butter over medium-high heat until the butter is just starting to sizzle. Pour in the egg mixture. (The egg mixture will begin to set immediately around the edge.) With an inverted pancake turner, carefully push the cooked portions at the edge toward the center, allowing the uncooked mixture to flow toward the surface of the pan. Tilt the pan and move the cooked portions as necessary so that the omelet is completely cooked. If you are filling the omelet, add the filling while the top is still moist and creamy-looking. With the pancake turner, fold the omelet in half or fold two sides in toward the center. Invert the omelet onto the plate with a quick flip of the wrist or slide the omelet from the pan onto a plate.

Makes 1 serving.

*Filling possibilities:*
You can create your own filling. Simply use one or two filling ingredients to total about 1/3 to 1/2 cup for each omelet. If you want to flavor the egg part itself, mix about 1/8 to 1/4 teaspoon of your favorite herb or spice into the egg mixture. You can use some raw vegetables and fruits as a filling, but to give the omelet a more finished flavor, sauté the vegetables and fruit in a small amount of butter in the omelet pan until they are tender. (You can also steam them.) Set them aside, cook the omelet, and then return them to the omelet.

To get you started, here are some ideas:

**Apple and Blue Cheese —** Sauté half a sliced small green apple in 2 teaspoons of butter until the apple is tender. Fill the almost cooked omelet with the cooked apple and 2 tablespoons of crumbled blue cheese and fold the omelet.

**Herbed Brie —** Add about 1/4 teaspoon total of dried thyme, basil, oregano, marjoram, or dill weed to the egg mixture. To the almost cooked omelet, add a slice or two of Brie and fold the omelet.

**Ham and Cheese —** Sprinkle the almost cooked omelet with 1/4 cup of finely chopped cooked ham and 1/4 cup of shredded cheese and fold the omelet.

**Broccoli and Cheese —** Sprinkle the almost cooked omelet with about 1/2 cup of cooked broccoli florets and 1/4 cup of shredded cheese and fold the omelet.

**Omelet Olé —** Top the almost cooked omelet with about 1/3 cup of salsa sauce, 1/4 cup of shredded Monterey Jack cheese, and 1/4 cup of shredded Cheddar cheese and fold the omelet. Spoon a tablespoon of low-fat sour cream on top.

**Pizza —** Add about 1/4 teaspoon of dried oregano to the egg mixture. Top the almost cooked omelet with 1/4 cup of tomato sauce, 1/4 cup of shredded mozzarella cheese, and 2 tablespoons of cooked mushrooms and fold the omelet.

## *Always a Bridesmaid . . . Never the Same Size*
# Low-Calorie Coleslaw

This coleslaw is made with a yogurt and reduced-calorie mayonnaise dressing. If you have any bell peppers, cut them into thin strips and add them to the slaw.

1 cup plain yogurt

3 tablespoons reduced-calorie
    mayonnaise

1/4 teaspoon salt

1/8 teaspoon Tabasco pepper sauce

2 cups thinly sliced or chopped
    green cabbage

2 cups thinly sliced or chopped red
    cabbage

1 cup grated carrot

In a large bowl, stir together the yogurt, mayonnaise, salt, and pepper sauce. Add the cabbages and carrot and toss gently to combine all the ingredients. Can be served chilled or at room temperature. Cover and refrigerate any leftovers.

Makes about 4 servings.

# *At the First Sign of Fall, the Dreaded Ski Pant Search Begins* **Easy Black Bean Soup**

Canned beans make this soup (souper easy) extra easy.  Add less broth if you want a thicker soup.  Serve it with a crusty whole grain bread and a tossed green salad.

**2 teaspoons olive oil**

**¹/₂ cup chopped onion**

**¹/₂ cup chopped green bell pepper**

**1 medium garlic clove, finely chopped**

**¹/₂ teaspoon ground cumin**

**1 (15-ounce) can black beans, drained**

**1 (13³/₄-ounce) can reduced-sodium chicken broth**

**Salt and freshly ground pepper to taste**

**Chopped tomatoes and/or reduced-fat sour cream (optional)**

In a medium saucepan over medium heat, heat the oil. Add the onion, green pepper, garlic, and cumin and cook, stirring frequently, for 5 to 7 minutes, or until the vegetables are softened.  Add the beans and chicken broth and cook until heated through.  Season with salt and pepper.  Serve in warmed bowls or mugs topped with chopped tomatoes and/or reduced-fat sour cream, if desired.

Makes 2 servings.

## *Who Needs a Five-Pound Box of Chocolate When You Have* **A Really Big Salad**

When you are looking for quantity and not calories, here's a jumbo salad to try. Substitute your own favorite vegetables or select those that look the best at the market. Top with sliced grilled chicken, canned water-packed drained tuna, drained beans, or a sliced hard-boiled egg to add extra substance to the salad.  Serve it with any of the following homemade salad dressings or use your favorite brand of reduced-calorie dressing. To make it easier and to avoid waste, select just the right amount of ingredients at a supermarket salad bar; top your creation with one of the following dressings.

**2 cups torn lettuce leaves**

**1 cup torn spinach leaves**

**6 cherry tomatoes, cut in half**

**6 mushrooms, rinsed and sliced**

**1 small carrot, grated**

**1/2 small cucumber, sliced**

**1/2 small red onion, chopped**

In a large bowl, gently toss all of the ingredients. Drizzle with one of the following salad dressings and serve.

Makes 1 jumbo serving.

# Skinny Dilled Dijon Yogurt Dressing

Use the basic mixture of yogurt and mayonnaise as the foundation for other flavors of dressings. This makes a fabulous dip for raw vegetables. For a thinner dressing, stir in a little skim milk until you achieve the consistency you desire.

**¹/₃ cup plain low-fat yogurt**

**¹/₃ cup reduced-calorie mayonnaise**

**¹/₄ cup chopped fresh parsley**

**2 tablespoons chopped fresh dill**

**2 teaspoons Dijon-style mustard**

**Salt and freshly ground black pepper to taste**

In a medium bowl, whisk together the yogurt, mayonnaise, parsley, dill, and mustard until combined. Season with salt and pepper. Cover and refrigerate the dressing until you are ready to serve it.

Makes about ⁷/₈ cup dressing.

# Svelte Chinese Dressing

**Add strips of grilled chicken, bean sprouts, and mandarin oranges to A Really Big Salad (page 40) along with this dressing to turn it into A Really Big Chinese Chicken Salad.**

**1/2 cup rice vinegar**

**3 tablespoons soy sauce**

**1 1/2 tablespoons finely chopped fresh ginger**

**1 tablespoon granulated sugar**

**1 tablespoon Dijon-style mustard**

**1 tablespoon oriental-style sesame oil**

**1 small garlic clove, finely chopped**

**Dash of Tabasco pepper sauce**

In a small container with a cover that fits tightly, combine all of the ingredients and shake to combine. Cover and refrigerate the dressing until you are ready to serve it.

Makes about 7/8 cup dressing.

# Creamy Thin Goddess Salad Dressing and Dip

Here's a thick dressing/dip that tastes substantial even though its calories are minimal. Serve it with crudités for weight watchers. It's also superb on top of baked potatoes.

1/2 cup fresh parsley leaves

1/2 cup fresh basil leaves

1 cup low-fat cottage cheese

2 tablespoons reduced-calorie mayonnaise

Freshly ground black pepper to taste

In the container of a blender or food processor fitted with a metal chopping blade, process the parsley and basil until finely chopped. Add the cottage cheese and mayonnaise and continue to process until the mixture is smooth. Season with pepper. Cover and refrigerate the dressing until you are ready to serve.

Makes about 1 1/4 cups dressing.

## 'Tis Better to Be Fit Than to Be Fried
# Three-Ingredient Unfried Chicken

This chicken stays moist because of its yogurt and bread crumb coating. Be extra virtuous and remove the skin of the chicken before you bake it. Bake a potato at the same time you cook the chicken. As it all bakes, munch on a few raw veggies. Serve it with a tossed salad or Low-Calorie Coleslaw (page 38).

**One broiler-fryer chicken (2 to 3 pounds), cut up into 8 pieces**

**1 cup plain yogurt**

**1 cup Italian-seasoned dry bread crumbs**

Preheat the oven to 375°F. If desired, remove the chicken's skin. Place the yogurt in a shallow bowl. Place the bread crumbs in a shallow plate.

Roll each piece of chicken first in the yogurt and then in the bread crumbs. Place the coated pieces of chicken in a baking pan. Bake for about 1 hour, or until the juices run clear when the chicken is pricked with the tines of a fork.

Makes 4 to 6 servings.

# *My Jeans Have Shrunk and Now So Must I* Southwest-Style Rice, Black Bean, Corn, and Pepper Salad

**Here's a satisfying colorful salad that is packed with fiber. A lime-juice-and-cilantro-based dressing adds lively flavor to the salad. It is great for toting in a plastic container for lunch. Serve it on a platter lined with lettuce leaves as perfect party food.**

**1/3 cup freshly squeezed lime juice**

**1 tablespoon olive oil**

**1/4 teaspoon Tabasco pepper sauce**

**1/4 teaspoon salt**

**3 cups cooked brown rice**

**1 can (15 ounces) black beans, drained and rinsed**

**1 cup cooked corn**

**1 cup chopped red bell pepper**

**1 cup chopped yellow bell pepper**

**1/4 cup chopped scallions**

**1/4 cup chopped cilantro**

**1 jalapeño pepper, seeded and finely chopped**

In a large bowl, stir together the lime juice, olive oil, pepper sauce, and salt. Add the rice, beans, corn, red pepper, yellow pepper, scallions, cilantro, and jalapeño pepper and toss gently to coat.

Makes about 7 cups salad; 4 servings.

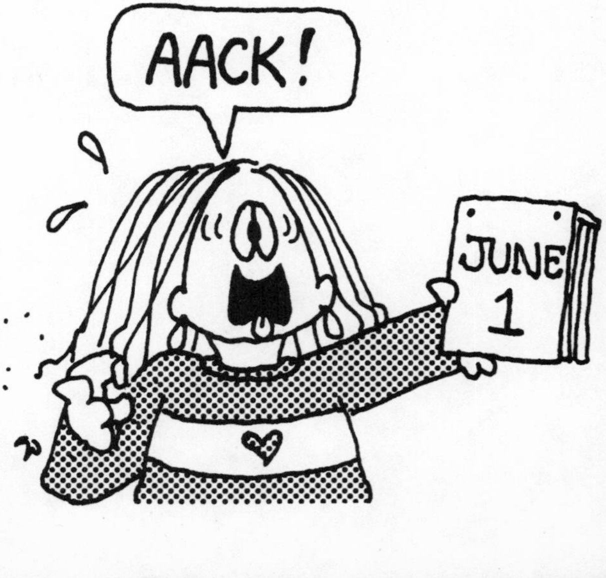
AACK!
JUNE
1

# *Nothing Encourages Revenge Like a High School Reunion* **Slim Fries**

**Here's a potato recipe that looks and tastes like the deep-fat fried variety. When you first get home from work, scrub the potatoes, slice them into ¹/₂-inch-wide strips, toss them into iced water, and preheat the oven. Then get changed and read the mail before popping the potato strips into the oven.**

**2 medium potatoes, unpeeled, scrubbed, and trimmed of any bruised spots**

**2 teaspoons butter, melted (in the microwave oven)**

**Salt and freshly ground pepper to taste**

Slice the potatoes lengthwise into ¹/₂-inch-thick strips. Place the strips of potatoes in a bowl of iced water for 20 minutes.

Meanwhile, preheat the oven to 450°F. Spray a baking sheet with nonstick vegetable or olive oil cooking spray. Drain the potatoes thoroughly and dry on paper towels.

Place the potatoes in a single layer on the prepared baking sheet. Brush with half of the melted butter. Bake for 20 minutes. Turn the potatoes, brush with the remaining butter and bake for 20 minutes longer, or until lightly browned. Sprinkle with salt and pepper.

Makes 1 large serving.

## *Why Did I Buy an Itsy-Bitsy, Teeny-Weeny Bikini* Linguine

Here's a pasta that's easy on the thighs. This recipe serves two. If it is just you eating, immediately put half of the mixture into an airtight container and refrigerate it to reheat and enjoy the next day. For a few extra calories, sprinkle a little grated Parmesan cheese on top.

**4 ounces thin linguine**

**1 tablespoon olive oil**

**1/2 cup chopped onion**

**1 medium garlic clove, finely chopped**

**Pinch of crushed red pepper flakes**

**1/4 teaspoon dried basil leaves, crushed**

**1/3 cup dry white wine**

**1 can (6 ounces) minced clams, undrained**

**3 tablespoons chopped fresh parsley**

**Salt and freshly ground black pepper to taste**

Cook the linguine according to the package directions and drain thoroughly.

Meanwhile, in a large skillet, heat the oil over medium heat. Add the onion, garlic, pepper flakes, and basil and cook, stirring frequently, for 4 to 6 minutes, or until the vegetables are tender.

Add the wine, increase the heat, and bring the mixture to a boil. Boil until about half of the liquid has evaporated. Add the clams and their liquid and continue cooking for about 2 to 3 minutes, or until heated through. Stir in the parsley. Add the drained linguine to the skillet and toss to coat with the clam mixture. Season with salt and pepper and serve.

Makes 2 servings.

## *AACK! He Wants to Go Tropical*
# Thin Thighs Turkey

This fresh-tasting recipe has captured the taste of Thailand using readily available American ingredients.  Use packaged turkey breast fillets for the turkey.  You can also use chicken breasts.

3/4 cup chicken broth

3 tablespoons chopped scallions (including tender green tops)

2 tablespoons chopped cilantro leaves

2 tablespoons soy sauce

1 tablespoon freshly squeezed lime juice

2 teaspoons cornstarch

2 teaspoons oriental-style sesame oil

1/2 pound turkey breast, cut into 2 by 1/4-inch strips

1/4 teaspoon crushed red pepper flakes

1 medium red bell pepper, seeded and cut into 2 by 1/4-inch strips (about 1 cup)

1 1/2 cups hot cooked rice

In a small bowl, stir together the chicken broth, scallions, cilantro, soy sauce, lime juice, and cornstarch and set aside.

In a nonstick wok or large skillet, heat the sesame oil over medium-high heat.  Add the turkey and crushed red pepper flakes and cook, stirring constantly, for 2 to 3 minutes.  Add the red pepper and cook for 2 minutes.  Stir the chicken broth mixture and add it to the wok.  Bring the mixture to a boil and cook for 1 minute to thicken the sauce.  Serve with the cooked rice.

Makes 2 servings.

# *Now That I've Committed to a Slinky Black Dress, I Have to Break Up with Ten Pounds* Balsamic Dijon Marinated Flank Steak

Flank steak is one of the leanest cuts of beef. This easy, flavorful marinade can be used with up to 3 pounds of other types of meat and poultry. Try it with pork chops. We recommend marinating the steak in a plastic bag as it takes up less room in the refrigerator. Of course, you can always allow the steak to stand in the marinade in a glass bowl.

**3/4 cup balsamic vinegar**

**2 tablespoons olive oil**

**2 tablespoons Dijon-style mustard**

**2 garlic cloves, finely chopped**

**1 teaspoon dried basil leaves, crushed**

**1/4 teaspoon Tabasco pepper sauce**

**1 flank steak, 1 to 3 pounds**

In a large freezer-weight plastic bag (or use two regular plastic bags, one inside the other), combine the vinegar, oil, mustard, garlic, basil, and pepper sauce. Add the flank steak and seal the bag. "Squish" the bag so that the mixture completely covers the steak. Place the bag in the refrigerator for 8 hours or overnight, occasionally turning the bag to distribute the marinade.

Position the grill or broiler rack about 5 inches from the heat source. Remove the steak from the marinade. Grill or broil the steak for 4 to 8 minutes on each side, or until cooked to the desired degree of doneness. If desired, brush the steak with the remaining marinade as it cooks. Thinly slice the steak diagonally across the grain.

Makes 4 to 6 servings.

# *In This Fast-Paced World of Greasy Take-Out Food, You Have to Stop and Smell the* **Lean Burgers**

**When nothing but a burger will do, here is this slimmed-down version that combines lean ground beef and ground turkey breast. Cook the number of burgers you need for dinner and individually wrap the rest of the burgers and freeze them for another day.**

**1 pound ground lean beef**

**1 pound ground turkey breast**

**2 cups chopped onions**

**2 tablespoons Worcestershire sauce**

**3/4 teaspoon dried thyme leaves, crushed**

**1/4 teaspoon dried oregano leaves, crushed**

**1/2 teaspoon salt**

**1/4 teaspoon freshly ground pepper**

**3 ounces thinly sliced part-skim mozzarella or other low-fat cheese**

**6 hamburger buns**

**6 lettuce leaves**

**6 slices of tomato**

Position the grill or broiler rack about 5 inches from the heat source.

In a large bowl, using a wooden spoon or your hands, mix together the beef, turkey, onions, Worcestershire sauce, thyme, oregano, salt, and pepper until combined. Shape the mixture into 6 patties.

Grill or broil the patties for 5 to 7 minutes on each side or until the burgers are cooked completely through. Top the burgers with the cheese and continue cooking about 30 seconds, or until the cheese melts. Place the burgers on the buns. Top with the lettuce and tomato and serve.

Makes 6 burgers.

# *I'm Invited to a Pool Party and I'd Rather Not Have to Wear the Table Tent* Grilled Tuna with Papaya Salsa

**Use this marinade and salsa with chicken or other types of fish, too!**

*Tuna:*

2 tablespoons freshly squeezed lime juice

1 teaspoon olive oil

1 small garlic clove, finely chopped

Dash of salt and freshly ground pepper

1 tuna steak, 1 to 1 1/2 inches thick (about 4 to 6 ounces)

*Papaya Salsa:*

1 ripe papaya, peeled, seeded, and chopped

1/2 medium red bell pepper, seeded and chopped

1/4 cup chopped red onion

1/4 cup chopped cilantro leaves

1/4 cup freshly squeezed lime juice

1/2 small jalapeño pepper, seeded and finely chopped

1/4 teaspoon salt

*To marinate the tuna:*
In a shallow dish, combine the lime juice, oil, garlic, salt, and pepper. Add the tuna steak and turn to coat it with the marinade. Cover and refrigerate it for up to 2 hours, or until you are ready to cook the tuna.

*To make the papaya salsa:*
Meanwhile, in a medium bowl, gently toss together all of the salsa ingredients to combine. Cover and refrigerate the salsa until you are ready to use it.

*To grill or broil the tuna:*
Position the grill or broiler rack about 5 inches from the heat source. Grill or broil the tuna steak for about 4 to 6 minutes on each side, or until the tuna is cooked to the desired degree of doneness. Serve with the salsa. Refrigerate any leftover salsa for another use.

Makes 1 serving plus extra salsa.

# *Just Because I'm Healthy Doesn't Mean I Have to Suffer* Low-Calorie Chocolate Sauce

A spoonful of this rich-tasting chocolate sauce will jazz up almost any dessert. Try it spooned over sliced bananas, strawberries, or Chocolate Angel Food Cake (page 56) for a low-fat dessert. Use a flavored liqueur, such as Chambord or Grand Marnier, in place of the vanilla for extra flavor. For espresso flavor, stir in a pinch of instant espresso powder.

**1/3 cup unsweetened cocoa powder**

**1/3 cup firmly packed brown sugar**

**2 teaspoons cornstarch**

**1 cup water**

**1 1/2 teaspoons vanilla extract**

In a medium saucepan, stir together the cocoa powder, brown sugar, and cornstarch until combined. Stir in the water and heat over medium-high heat, stirring constantly, until the mixture comes to a boil. Boil for 1 minute to thicken the sauce. Stir in the vanilla. Cover and refrigerate any leftovers.

Makes 1 1/2 cups sauce.

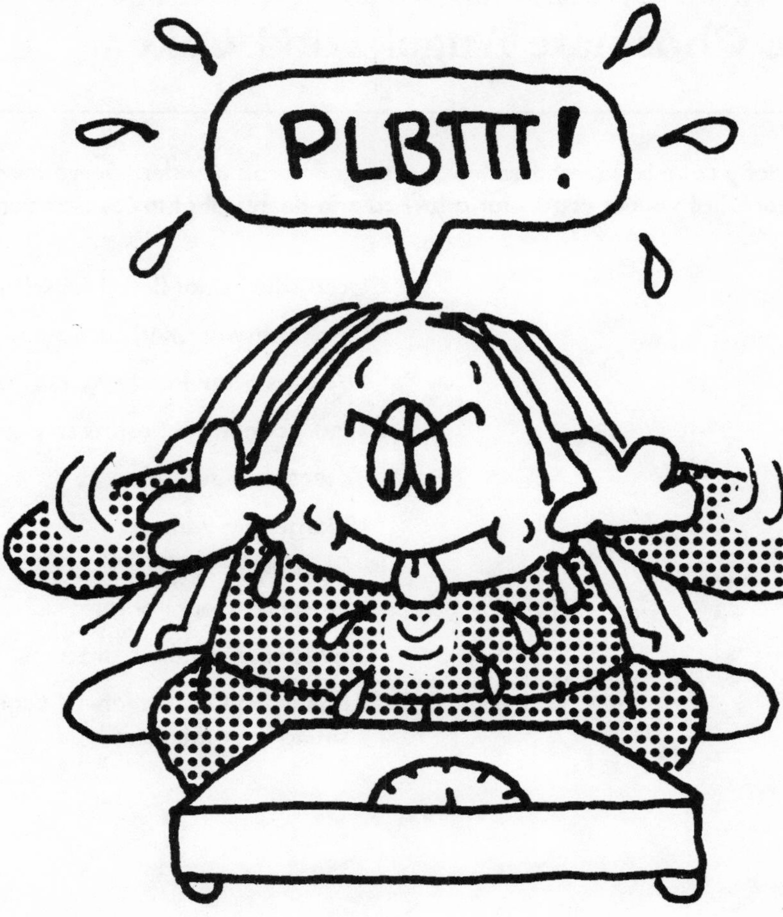
PLBTTT!

# *I Refuse to be Victimized by the Gene Pool*
# Fat-Free Chocolate Angel Food Cake

This moist and lofty cake is flavored with espresso and cocoa powder. Serve it with fresh fruit and a spoonful of vanilla yogurt for a low-calorie dessert that tastes decadent!

1 cup sifted cake flour (not self-rising)

1/3 cup unsweetened cocoa powder

1 1/4 cups granulated sugar

1 teaspoon instant espresso powder

1/4 teaspoon salt

12 large egg whites,
   at room temperature

1 teaspoon cream of tartar

2 teaspoons vanilla extract

1 tablespoon confectioners' sugar for
   sifting over the cake

Position a rack in the bottom third of the oven and preheat the oven to 350°F.

In a medium bowl, stir together the flour, cocoa powder, 1/2 cup of the granulated sugar, espresso powder, and salt. Sift the mixture onto a piece of waxed paper.

In a grease-free, large bowl, using a handheld electric mixer set at medium speed, beat the egg whites for 20 to 30 seconds, or until foamy. Beat in the cream of tartar. Gradually increase the speed to high and continue beating until soft peaks start to form. Beat in the vanilla. Two tablespoons at a time, beat in the remaining 3/4 cup of granulated sugar. In three additions, sift the flour/cocoa mixture over the surface of the beaten egg whites, and using a rubber spatula, gently fold in each addition just until combined.

Scrape the batter into a grease-free 9-inch (14-cup) tube pan and gently smooth the surface. With a long knife, cut through the batter to remove any large air bubbles. Bake for 40 to 50 minutes, or until the top is dry and it springs back when touched lightly with your fingertip.

Invert the cake to cool. If the pan does not have "stands," invert the cake over a funnel or the neck of a soda bottle. Cool for about 1 1/2 hours. Loosen the cake with a metal spatula and invert it onto a serving plate. Sift the confectioners' sugar evenly over the cake.

Makes 12 servings.

# Sweat Suit Food

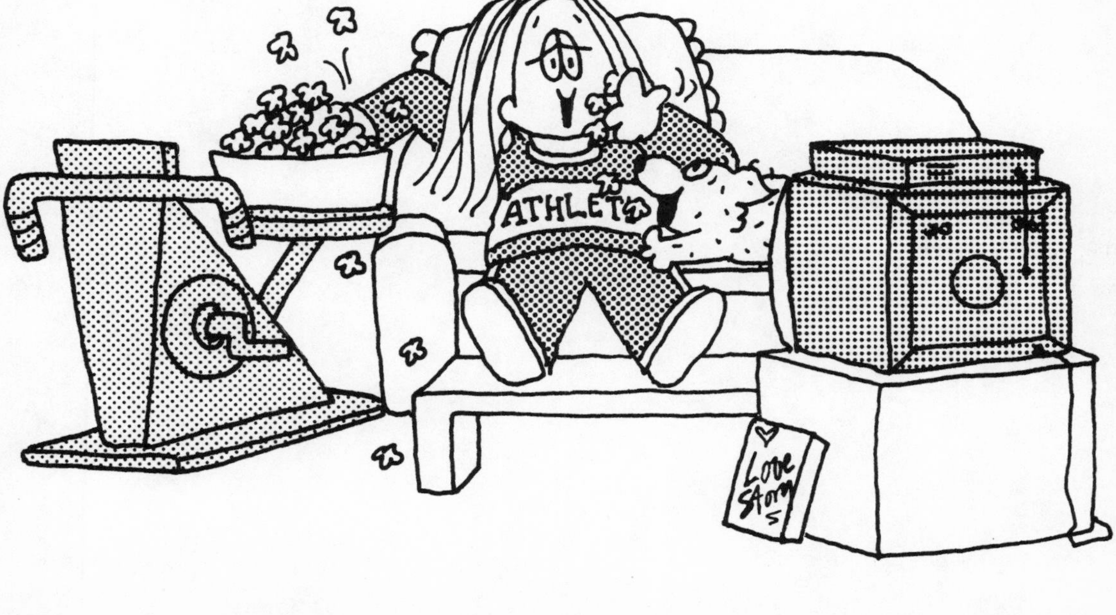
ATHLET
Love Story

# Sweat Suit Food

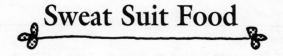

Men take a taste and leave the rest. Women take a taste and eat the whole pie. Men date. Women turn it into a relationship. It's as simple as that.

For all their pregame bags of chips and halftime sandwiches, men will never truly understand one of the most nurturing, cozy, happy concepts of life: food as companion.

Not to be confused with revenge food or self-pity food, Sweat Suit Food is simply what we need to eat sometimes when we just want to curl up with a good friend, but don't necessarily want another human being in the room.

This is food you could be proud to serve to company sometime, but will be positively delirious to serve to yourself anytime.

It's a vacation from stress, a time-out from the diet, the "I'm worth it, I deserve it, I-don't-want-to-talk-about-it-just-let-me-eat" kind of food you pray will be waiting for you in your refrigerator every time you open the door.

And, needless to say, it's all the more delicious when you eat it while lying on the couch wearing clothes designed for intense exercise.

## *Turn Out the Lights, Pop in a Movie, and Pass the Bowl* **Parmesan Popcorn**

A simple sprinkling of Parmesan cheese on popcorn turns it into an extra-special salty snack!  Make your favorite type of popcorn — homemade or microwave — and adjust the amount of Parmesan according to the saltiness of the popcorn and your personal taste. (The cheese will not stick as well to air-popped or nonfat popcorn.)

**8 cups popped popcorn**

**¹/₄ to ¹/₂ cup grated Parmesan cheese, to taste**

In a large bowl, toss together the popcorn and the Parmesan cheese to combine.

Makes 2 servings.

# *I Need the Afternoon to Rearrange My Closet and Make Room for the New Clothing I Plan to Purchase* Sassy Salsa Guacamole

**If you want to speed up the ripening of your avocado, place it in a paper bag for a few days.**

1 medium-size ripe avocado, skin and pit removed

3 medium-size ripe tomatoes, finely chopped

¼ cup chopped scallions (including tender green tops)

3 tablespoons chopped cilantro

1 medium serrano or other hot chile pepper, trimmed, seeded, and finely chopped

2 tablespoons freshly squeezed lime juice

1 garlic clove, minced

½ teaspoon salt

In a medium bowl, mash the avocado. Stir in the tomatoes, scallions, cilantro, pepper, lime, garlic, and salt. Cover. Chill until ready to serve. Serve with chips, cut-up fresh vegetables, or Toasted Parmesan Pita Triangles (page 87).

Makes 3¼ cups dip.

# *This is the Perfect Evening to Lock Ourselves In and Try on All Our Makeup Samples* Crab Cakes with Red Pepper Tartar Sauce

These crab cakes are substantial enough to be a main course, yet they could also be used as a first course.  Try them served in a roll as a delicious "burger."

### Crab Cakes:

1 pound crabmeat, well picked over (or use frozen, thawed, and drained crab)

2 large eggs, lightly beaten

2 tablespoons mayonnaise

2 tablespoons chopped fresh parsley

2 tablespoons chopped scallions (including tender green tops)

1 tablespoon freshly squeezed lemon juice

1/4 teaspoon salt

1/4 teaspoon Tabasco pepper sauce

1 cup crushed soda crackers

1 to 2 tablespoons olive oil

1 to 2 tablespoons unsalted butter

### Red Pepper Tartar Sauce:

1 cup finely chopped red bell pepper

1/4 cup finely chopped scallions (including tender green tops)

1/2 cup mayonnaise

1/2 cup sour cream

1 tablespoon freshly squeezed lemon juice

1 tablespoon chopped fresh parsley

Generous dash of Tabasco pepper sauce

*To make the crab cakes:*
In a large bowl, gently stir together the crab, eggs, mayonnaise, parsley, scallions, lemon juice, salt, and pepper sauce. Stir in the crushed crackers.

Using about 1/2 cup of crab mixture per cake, form the mixture into about six cakes that are each about 4 inches across and about 3/4 inch thick.

In a large skillet, heat 1 tablespoon of the oil and 1 tablespoon of the butter over medium-high heat. Add as many crab cakes as will fit into the skillet and cook for 3 to 5 minutes on each side or until they are lightly browned and cooked through. Repeat until all the crab cakes are cooked. Add additional oil and butter to the skillet as necessary to keep the crab cakes from sticking. Drain well on paper towels.

*To make the red pepper tartar sauce:*
Meanwhile, in a medium bowl, stir together all of the tartar sauce ingredients until combined. Cover and refrigerate until ready to serve.

Makes 6 crab cakes and about 2 cups sauce.

# I'm Having My Own Little Fiesta at Home **Enchiladas**

This is a loose adaptation of a true enchilada that captures all the craved-for flavors of old Mexico — easily! If you have extra cooked chicken or beef, add it to the filling of this enchilada. Try it with Sassy Salsa Guacamole (page 63).

3/4 cup refried beans

1 cup picante sauce

1 tablespoon chopped drained bottled jalapeño peppers

1 tablespoon chopped scallions (including tender green top)

1/4 teaspoon ground cumin

One 10-inch diameter flour tortilla

1/2 cup shredded Cheddar cheese

1/2 cup shredded Monterey Jack cheese

1 cup shredded lettuce

1/3 cup chopped tomatoes

Sour cream for garnish (optional)

Preheat the oven to 350°F. In a small bowl, stir together the beans, 1/4 cup of the picante sauce, jalapeños, scallions, and cumin until combined.

Place the tortilla on a work surface. Place the bean mixture down the center of the tortilla. Top the mixture with half of the Cheddar cheese and half of the Monterey Jack cheese. Roll the sides of the tortilla over the filling and place the filled enchilada in a small baking dish (a loaf pan works well), seam side down.

Spoon the remaining 3/4 cup of picante sauce over the enchilada. Sprinkle with the remaining 1/4 cup of Cheddar cheese and 1/4 cup of Monterey Jack cheese. Bake for 20 to 25 minutes, or until heated through. Remove enchilada from the oven and transfer to a plate. Smother the enchilada with the lettuce and tomatoes. Garnish with sour cream, if desired.

Makes 1 serving.

## *Swimsuits Are Way Overrated* **Boboli Olé**

**Use store-bought bread shells to make pizza in a flash. Here's one that combines popular Mexican-flavored ingredients.**

**¹/₃ cup salsa sauce**

**One 6-inch Italian bread shell**

**¹/₄ cup shredded Cheddar cheese**

**¹/₄ cup shredded Monterey Jack cheese**

Preheat the oven to 450°F.

Spread the salsa sauce evenly over the surface of the bread shell. Sprinkle the cheeses over the salsa. Bake for 10 to 12 minutes, or until the pizza is heated through and the cheeses are bubbly.

Makes 1 serving.

## *I Need Some Quality Time with My Dog* Sky-High Scone-Crusted Pizza

Here's an easy pizza with a crust that is simply leavened with baking powder. Chopped walnuts and whole wheat flour make the base extra interesting. We've topped this pie with broccoli, roasted red peppers, and goat cheese along with traditional shredded mozzarella cheese, which gives this pie its towering proportions. Of course, you can use your favorite pizza toppings.

**Dough:**

3/4 cup whole wheat flour

3/4 cup all-purpose flour

3 tablespoons finely chopped walnuts

1 1/2 teaspoons baking powder

1/8 teaspoon salt

1/4 cup (1/2 stick) unsalted butter, chilled and cut into 1/2-inch cubes

1/4 cup milk

1 large egg

**Topping:**

2 teaspoons olive oil

1/2 teaspoon dried basil leaves, crushed

1/4 teaspoon dried oregano leaves, crushed

1 (10-ounce) package thawed frozen broccoli flowerets, drained

1/2 cup strips of homemade or drained bottled roasted red peppers (see Note)

4 ounces goat cheese, cut into 1/2-inch pieces

1/4 cup coarsely broken walnuts

8 ounces shredded mozzarella cheese

Preheat the oven to 400°F. Lightly butter or spray with nonstick vegetable cooking spray an 11-inch-diameter circle in the center of a baking sheet or pizza pan.

In a large bowl, stir together the flours, chopped walnuts, baking powder, and salt. Distribute the butter cubes evenly over the flour mixture. With your fingertips, quickly press the butter and flour mixture together until the mixture resembles coarse crumbs. In a small bowl, stir together the milk and egg. Add the liquid mixture to the dry ingredients and stir to combine until the mixture pulls together.

With lightly floured hands, pat the dough into a 10-inch-diameter circle in the center of the prepared baking sheet.

Brush the surface of the dough with the olive oil. Sprinkle the basil and oregano evenly over the top.

Evenly distribute the broccoli, red pepper strips, goat cheese, and broken walnuts over the surface. Sprinkle the mozzarella cheese over the top. Bake for 20 to 25 minutes, or until the cheese is melted and the crust is lightly browned.

Remove from the baking sheet to a wire rack. Cut the pizza into wedges and serve.

Makes 2 generous servings.

Note: *To roast a pepper, position the broiler pan 5 to 6 inches from the heat source. Preheat the broiler. Place the pepper on the broiler pan. Broil the pepper, turning it, until the skin is lightly and evenly charred. Place the pepper in a bowl and cover the bowl with plastic wrap. When the pepper is cool, rub away the burnt skin. Stem and core the pepper.*

# *I'd Go to the Gym but I Seem to Have Misplaced My Energy* Artichoke Mushroom Tortellini Salad

Here's an easy recipe that's great for dinner one day and for toting as a lunch the next. Using marinated artichokes and their liquid for the dressing keeps this recipe extra easy. If the salad stands and needs more dressing, add a little olive oil and red wine vinegar. You can use other flavors of tortellini if that is what you have on hand.

1 package (9 ounces) refrigerated mushroom tortellini

1 jar (6 ounces) marinated artichoke hearts with liquid

1/2 cup slivered drained oil-packed sun-dried tomatoes

4 ounces smoked turkey, cut into slivers

1/2 cup sliced pitted ripe olives

Grated Parmesan cheese (optional)

Cook the tortellini according to the package directions and drain thoroughly.

In a large bowl, gently toss together the hot tortellini, artichokes (with their liquid), tomatoes, turkey, and olives. Sprinkle with Parmesan cheese, if desired. This is good at room temperature or refrigerated. Cover and refrigerate leftovers.

Makes 2 servings.

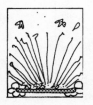

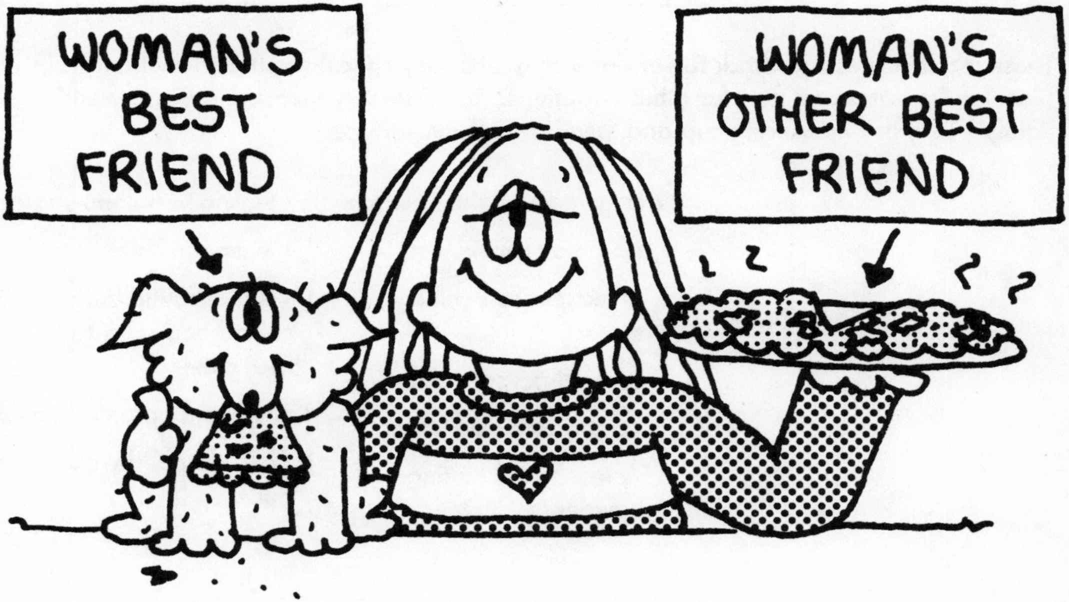
WOMAN'S BEST FRIEND
WOMAN'S OTHER BEST FRIEND

# *It's Saturday Night and I'm Wearing My Robe* **Date Nut Scones**

These moist scones are chock full of dates and nuts. Try chocolate chips and dried fruits in place of the dates and nuts for other variations. To accurately measure flour, spoon it lightly into a dry measuring cup and then level off the surface.

2 large eggs, lightly beaten

1/2 cup buttermilk

1 1/2 teaspoons vanilla extract

2 cups all-purpose flour

1/3 cup granulated sugar

1 1/2 teaspoons baking powder

1/2 teaspoon baking soda

1/4 teaspoon salt

1/3 cup unsalted butter, chilled and cut into 1/2-inch cubes

1 cup chopped pitted dates

1/3 cup chopped walnuts or pecans

Preheat the oven to 400°F. Lightly butter a baking sheet.

Reserve 1 tablespoon of the eggs for brushing on top of the scones. In a medium bowl, stir together the buttermilk, remaining eggs, and vanilla.

In a large bowl, stir together the flour, sugar, baking powder, baking soda, and salt. With a pastry blender or two knives used scissors fashion, cut in the butter until the mixture resembles coarse crumbs. Stir the buttermilk mixture into the flour mixture until combined. Stir in the dates and nuts. Turn the dough out onto a lightly floured surface and knead it for 30 to 60 seconds, or until combined.

On the floured surface, pat the dough out into a 6-inch square. Cut the dough into 2-inch squares. Transfer the scones to the prepared baking sheet and brush the tops with the reserved egg. Bake for 14 to 17 minutes, or until the scones are lightly browned.

Transfer the baking sheet to a wire rack and cool for 5 minutes. Using a spatula, transfer the scones to the wire rack and cool. Serve warm.

Makes 9 scones.

# *I Love Workout Clothes . . . They Have Such Stretchy Waistbands* Good Old-Fashioned Spaghetti and Meatballs

If you don't have the time or energy to make meatballs, the sauce is good all by itself over pasta.

*Tomato Sauce:*

1 tablespoon olive oil

1 cup chopped onion

1 medium garlic clove, finely chopped

1 can (28 ounces) Italian-style tomatoes, chopped, with their juice

1 can (16 ounces) tomato sauce

1/4 cup tomato paste

1 small bay leaf

1 teaspoon dried basil leaves, crushed

1/4 teaspoon dried oregano leaves, crushed

1/4 teaspoon salt

1/8 teaspoon freshly ground pepper

*Meatballs:*

1 pound ground beef

1/2 cup Italian-seasoned dry bread crumbs

1 large egg, lightly beaten

2 medium garlic cloves, finely chopped

1/2 teaspoon salt

1/8 teaspoon freshly ground pepper

2 tablespoons olive oil

12 ounces spaghetti

*To make the tomato sauce:*
In a large saucepan, heat the olive oil over medium-high heat. Add the onion and garlic and cook for 7 to 10 minutes, stirring occasionally, until the onion is softened. Add the tomatoes and their juice, tomato sauce, tomato paste, bay leaf, basil, oregano, salt, and pepper. Reduce the heat and simmer, stirring occasionally, for about 30 minutes.

*To make the meatballs:*
Meanwhile, in a large bowl, gently mix together the ground beef, bread crumbs, egg, garlic, salt, and pepper until combined. Shape the mixture into about eighteen meatballs, using about 2 table-spoons of mixture for each one.

In a large skillet, heat the oil over medium-high heat. Add the meatballs and cook for 4 to 6 minutes, turning to brown all the surfaces. With a slotted spoon, transfer the meatballs to paper towels to drain. Add the meatballs to the tomato sauce. Simmer gently for 15 minutes. Remove and discard the bay leaf from the sauce.

Meanwhile, cook the pasta according to the package directions and drain thoroughly. Add the meatballs and sauce to the spaghetti and serve.

Makes 6 servings.

## *The Four-and-a-Half-Hour, Five-Phone Call* Chocolate Chunk Cherry Almond Bread Pudding

**It's easy to pick away at this entire dish — whether you are picking at the crusty top or going after a chewy cherry, a melting square of chocolate, or a toasted almond sliver...**

5 large eggs

3/4 cup firmly packed brown sugar

3 cups milk

1 tablespoon almond extract

1 loaf (about 10 ounces) Italian or French bread, cut into 1-inch cubes (about 12 cups cubes)

1 cup dried cherries

9 ounces bittersweet chocolate, cut into 1/2-inch pieces

1/2 cup slivered almonds

Preheat the oven to 325°F. Butter or lightly spray a 13 by 9 by 2-inch baking dish with nonstick vegetable cooking spray.

In a large bowl, whisk together the eggs until combined. Whisk in the brown sugar. Whisk in the milk and almond extract until blended.

Add the bread cubes and toss to moisten the cubes with the mixture. Gently stir in the cherries, bittersweet chocolate, and almonds. Scrape the mixture into the prepared dish. Bake for 45 to 50 minutes, or until the mixture is set. Serve warm. Cover and refrigerate any leftovers for up to five days. Reheat to serve.

Makes 8 to 10 servings.

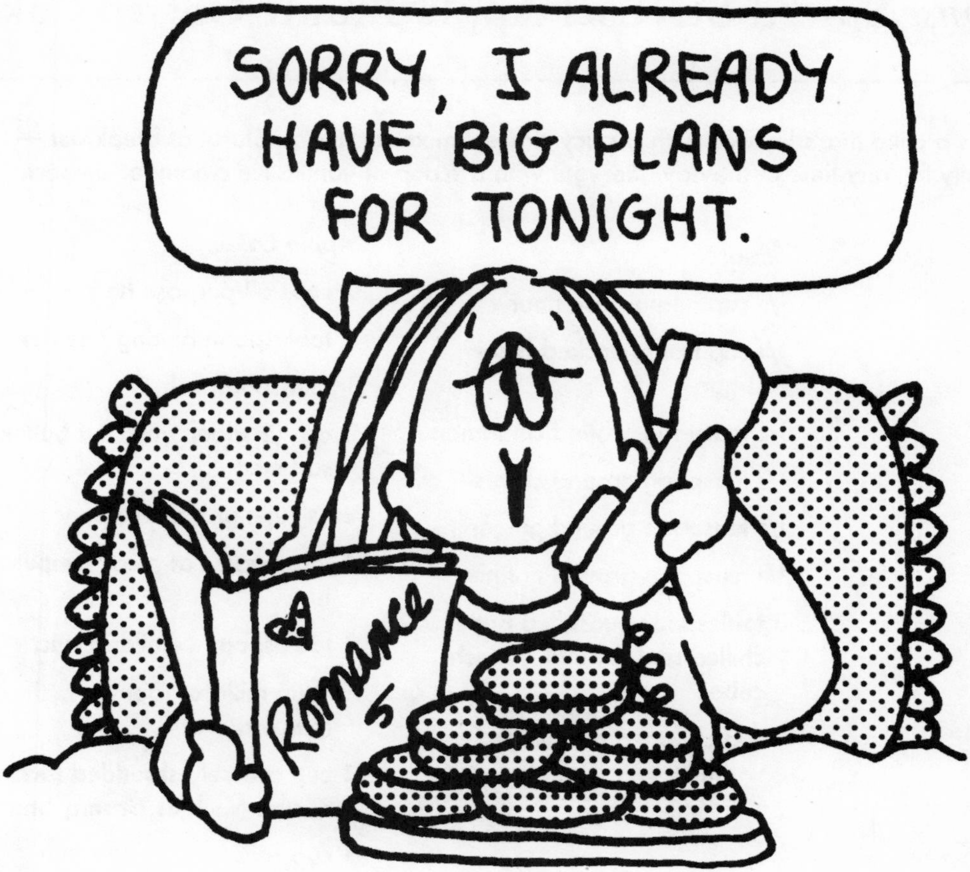
SORRY, I ALREADY HAVE BIG PLANS FOR TONIGHT.
Romance

# *I Woke Up Late Anyway So Why Bother Leaving the House* Spiced Streusel Apple Bundt Coffee Cake

Here's a cake that's layered with a spicy streusel mixture. It's a natural at breakfast — actually for any time of the day. Serve it with a scoop of vanilla ice cream for dessert.

### Streusel:

1/3 cup all-purpose flour

1/4 cup firmly packed brown sugar

1/2 teaspoon ground cinnamon

1/8 teaspoon ground cloves

1/8 teaspoon ground ginger

1/8 teaspoon ground nutmeg

3 tablespoons unsalted butter, chilled and cut into 1/2-inch cubes

1 cup chopped pecans or walnuts

### Apple Cake:

3 cups all-purpose flour

1 tablespoon baking powder

1/2 teaspoon salt

1 cup (2 sticks) unsalted butter, softened

1 1/2 cups granulated sugar

4 large eggs, at room temperature

1 tablespoon vanilla extract

1/4 cup milk, at room temperature

1 cup coarsely shredded tart apples (such as Granny Smith)

1 cup raisins

Confectioners' sugar for sifting over the top of the cake (optional)

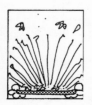

*To make the streusel:*
In a medium bowl, stir together the flour, brown sugar, cinnamon, cloves, ginger, and nutmeg. Add the butter cubes. Using your fingertips, quickly rub the butter into the flour mixture until the mixture resembles coarse crumbs. Stir in the nuts and set aside.

*To make the apple cake:*
Preheat the oven to 325°F. Butter a 10-inch Bundt cake pan. Dust the pan with flour and tap out the excess.

In a medium bowl, stir together the flour, baking powder, and salt. In a large bowl, using a handheld electric mixer, beat together the butter and sugar until combined. One at a time, beat in the eggs, beating well after each addition. Beat in the vanilla. In three additions each, alternately beat in the flour mixture and the milk, beating just until combined. Beat in the apples. Using a wooden spoon, stir in the raisins.

Sprinkle about one third of the streusel evenly over the bottom of the prepared pan. Spoon half of the batter over the streusel and spread evenly. Sprinkle the batter evenly with another one third of the streusel. Spoon the remaining batter over the streusel and spread evenly. Sprinkle the remaining one third of the streusel evenly over the top. Bake for 65 to 75 minutes, or until a cake tester or toothpick inserted into the center of the cake comes out clean and the cake is lightly golden.

Transfer the pan to a wire rack. Cool for 10 minutes. Carefully invert the cake onto the rack and cool completely. Sift confectioners' sugar over the top of the cake, if desired. Store the cake in an airtight container at cool room temperature. Can be stored up to 5 days.

Makes 16 to 20 servings.

## *Laundry Night*
# Chocolate Chunk Macadamia Nut Cookies

When the laundry calls, the name of the game is sustenance and convenience. These decadent cookies fill the bill perfectly!

2 1/4 cups all-purpose flour

3/4 teaspoon baking powder

1/4 teaspoon salt

1 cup (2 sticks) unsalted butter, softened

3/4 cup firmly packed brown sugar

1/2 cup granulated sugar

2 large eggs, at room temperature

2 teaspoons vanilla extract

12 ounces bittersweet or semi-sweet chocolate, cut into 1/2-inch pieces

1 1/4 cups chopped lightly salted macadamia nuts

In a large bowl, stir together the flour, baking powder, and salt. In another large bowl, using a wooden spoon, cream together the butter and sugars. One at a time, add the eggs to the butter-sugar mixture, stirring well after each addition. Stir in the vanilla. Gradually stir in the flour mixture until combined. Stir in the chocolate chunks and nuts. Cover and refrigerate the dough for at least 2 hours or overnight.

Preheat the oven to 300°F. Using a 1/4-cup measuring cup, drop the dough by cupfuls onto an ungreased baking sheet, leaving at least 2 inches between the dough mounds. Bake one sheet at a time, for 30 to 35 minutes, or until the cookies are lightly browned. Remove the baking sheet to a wire rack and cool for 5 minutes. Using a metal spatula, transfer the cookies to wire racks and cool completely. Repeat until all the dough is used. When cool, store the cookies in an airtight container for up to 2 weeks.

These cookies freeze well for up to 3 months.

Makes about 22 cookies.

# A Good Book, a Glass of Milk, and Thou Banana Bread

**It seems that bananas are either too green or they've become a major attraction for flies. Here's an easy recipe for banana bread to use those bananas that are soft and speckled with brown spots.**

1 3/4 cups all-purpose flour

1 teaspoon baking powder

1/2 teaspoon baking soda

1/4 teaspoon salt

1/2 cup (1 stick) unsalted butter, softened

3/4 cup granulated sugar

2 large eggs, at room temperature

1 cup mashed ripe bananas (about 2 large bananas)

3 tablespoons milk

2 teaspoons vanilla extract

1/2 cup chopped walnuts or pecans (optional)

Preheat the oven to 350°F. Butter or lightly coat with non-stick vegetable cooking spray an 8 1/2-by-4 1/2-by-2 1/4-inch loaf pan.

In a large bowl, stir together the flour, baking powder, baking soda, and salt. In another bowl, and using a wooden spoon, cream together the butter and sugar until blended. One at a time, add the eggs, beating well after each addition. Add the bananas, milk, and vanilla and stir just until combined. (The mixture may look curdled.) Stir in the flour mixture just until blended. Stir in the nuts, if desired.

Scrape the batter into the prepared pan and spread evenly. Bake for 45 to 55 minutes, or until a cake tester inserted into the center of the bread comes out clean and the bread is slightly browned.

Remove the pan to a wire rack. Cool for 10 minutes before removing the bread from the pan; finish cooling on the rack. Store the completely cooled bread in an airtight container at cool room temperature.

Makes 1 loaf; 12 to 16 slices.

# Grown-Up Food

# Grown-Up Food

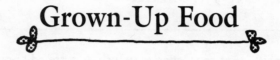

Like many dynamic, successful women of my generation, I always fantasized that, one day, I would entertain groups of witty, intelligent friends in my home.

The day came and went and all I had to serve my guests was a half-eaten bag of low-sodium taco chips. "Where's the food?" I wondered. "Where are the chic hors d'oeuvres?" "What sort of hostess would invite people to her home and make them root through the cupboards for their own refreshments??!"

It was only when I began arm-wrestling one of my guests for the last diet soda that I realized with horror that we were, in fact, in my home. That I was the hostess. And that, shockingly, it was my turn to be the grown-up.

If the fact that I was in charge wasn't frightening enough, it was immediately followed by the realization that even if I had thought to prepare something, I wouldn't have had the slightest idea what to fix.

Armed with the following dishes, I have since learned that being the gown-up requires only a few basic ingredients:

1. a great recipe
2. a good attitude
3. lots of time left over to hide the dirty pans in the garage and obsess about your hair.

# *AACK! They're Coming in Twenty-Three Minutes*
## Red Pepper Dip/Spread

This versatile and sophisticated concoction is superb as a speedy party dip but also works well as a topper for canapés. Trim the crust from slices of hearty whole grain bread and spread each slice with a 1/8-inch-thick layer of spread. Cut each slice into quarters and then cut each quarter in half to form two triangles. If desired, decorate each piece with slivers of roasted red pepper, ripe olives, or chives. For Valentine's Day, when entertaining that special someone, cut the bread into heart shapes using a metal cookie cutter. This rosy spread is also great as a sandwich spread on hearty whole grain bread or a bagel.

1/4 cup drained oil-packed sun-dried tomatoes, oil reserved

1 medium garlic clove, finely chopped

1 jar (7 ounces) roasted red peppers, drained

3 to 5 drops Tabasco pepper sauce

1 package (8 ounces) Neufchâtel or cream cheese, softened

In a small skillet, cook garlic in 2 teaspoons of the reserved oil for 2 to 4 minutes, or until the garlic is softened.

In the container of a food processor fitted with a metal chopping blade, process the tomatoes, garlic mixture, red peppers, and pepper sauce until smooth (with small pieces of tomato remaining). Add the Neufchâtel and process with an on-and-off motion until the mixture is blended. Scrape the mixture into a small bowl and serve immediately with Toasted Parmesan Pita Triangles (page 87), crackers, chips, and/or raw vegetable dippers. Cover and refrigerate any leftovers for up to 5 days.

Makes about 2 cups dip.

# *I'm Throwing a Party and Forgot to Plan a Menu*
# Toasted Parmesan Pita Triangles

**These flavorful breads are a simple snack on their own but are delicious as "dippers" for almost any kind of dip.**

**Pita bread**

**Olive oil**

**Grated Parmesan cheese**

Preheat the oven to 350°F. Split each pita bread horizontally into two rounds. Lightly brush the rough sides with olive oil. Sprinkle a thin layer of Parmesan cheese over the olive oil.

Cut each pita round into wedges (the number depends on the diameter of pita bread that you are using). Arrange the triangles on a baking sheet and bake for 5 to 10 minutes, or until lightly toasted. Serve with dips or as an accompaniment with soups and salads. Store leftover triangles in an airtight container at cool room temperature up to 5 days.

# *I Only Have Time for Half a Shower, One Coat of Nail Polish, and Two Ingredients* Party Brie

Here's a super easy party recipe. Place the plate that held the cheese while it was being heated in the center of a larger platter. Surround it with small clusters of grapes or crackers and slices of French bread for an attractive presentation. Of course, you can scale this recipe down accordingly to work with a small wheel of Brie.

**1 wheel (1 kilo) of Brie**

**3/4 cup chopped drained oil-packed sun-dried tomatoes**

Place the Brie on a microwave-safe plate large enough to hold the cheese and small enough to fit into your microwave oven. It's helpful if the plate has a rim. Using a sharp knife, trim off the top crust (about 1/4 inch) from the cheese.

Scatter the chopped tomatoes evenly over the cut surface of the cheese. Cover the tomato-topped cheese with plastic wrap and microwave on high for 2 to 4 minutes, or until the cheese is melted. Serve the cheese with crackers and slices of bread. If the cheese gets cool and firm, return it to the microwave oven and cook it for 1 to 2 minutes longer, or until it is soft again.

Makes 10 to 12 servings.

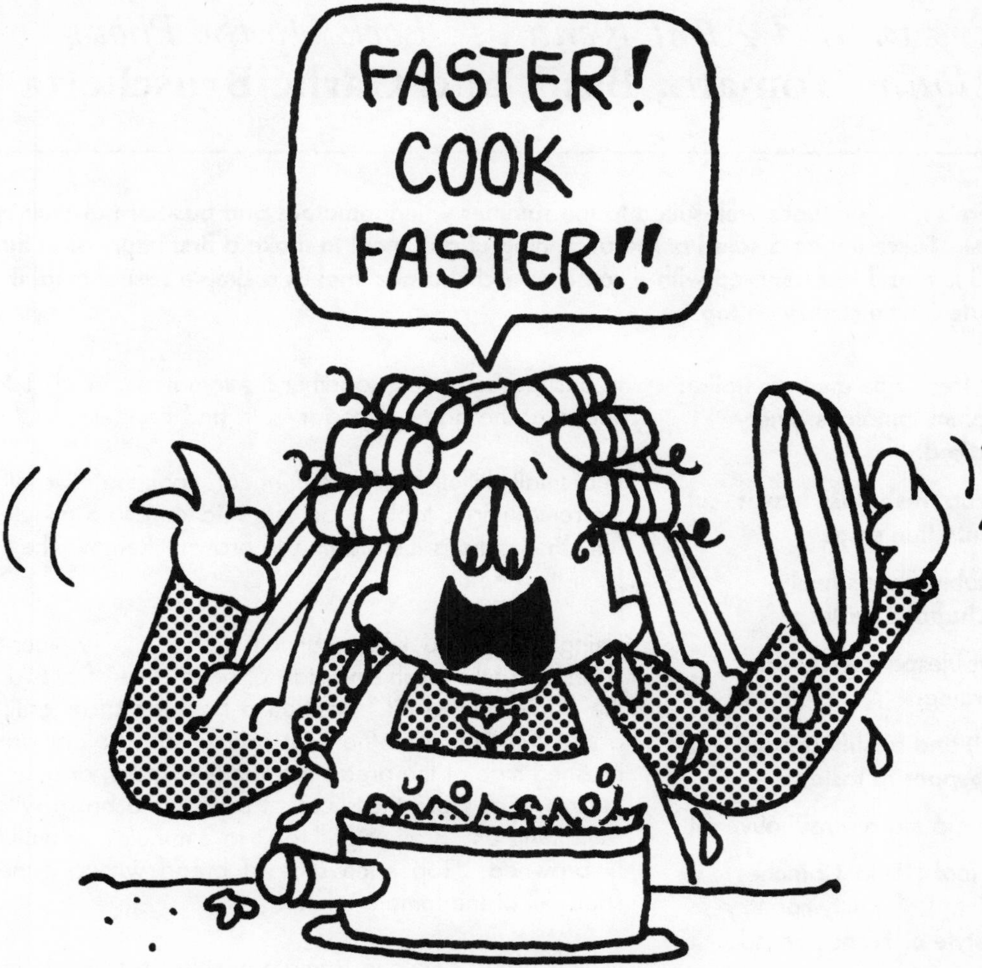
FASTER! COOK FASTER!!

## *I've Invited Aunt Rena . . . Lock Up the Photo Albums* Tomato, Basil, and Garlic Bruschetta

Here's a recipe that's well-suited to the summer when tomatoes and basil are at their very best. Serve it with a salad at the beginning of any meal to make a first impression that will last and last. Served with a salad, bruschetta also makes a simple casual meal if you grate a little cheese on top.

12 fresh ripe medium Italian plum tomatoes, finely diced

1 cup fresh basil leaves, cut into thin strips

2 tablespoons finely chopped garlic

1 tablespoon red wine vinegar

Salt and freshly ground pepper to taste

1/4 cup extra-virgin olive oil

1 loaf (10 to 12 inches long) of crusty country-style or French bread

In a large bowl, toss together the tomatoes, basil, 1 tablespoon of the garlic, vinegar, salt, and pepper.

In a small skillet, over medium heat, cook the olive oil and the remaining 1 tablespoon of garlic for 2 to 3 minutes, or until the garlic is just starting to brown. Remove the skillet from the heat.

Using a serrated knife, cut the bread into 3/4-inch-thick slices. Lightly brush one side of each slice of bread with the garlic-infused oil. Position a broiler pan or grill rack about 6 inches from the heat source and broil or grill the brushed side of the bread for 1 to 2 minutes, or until lightly browned. Turn the slices of bread and brush with the remaining oil. Broil or grill for 1 to 2 minutes, or until lightly browned. Top each slice of bread with a generous spoonful of the tomato mixture.

Makes about 4 1/2 cups tomato mixture; 6 to 8 servings.

# *His Old Girlfriend Will be There . . . I Hear She's Allergic to Cheese* Quick Jalapeño Cheese Quesadilla with Southwest Salsa

Use any leftover black beans from making the salsa to sprinkle over salads or as an ingredient in soup. Southwestern-style salsa (including corn and black beans) is available in many areas of the United States. Add chopped fresh scallions and cilantro for a livelier made-from-scratch taste.

**Southwest Salsa:**

1 jar (11 ounces) tomato salsa

1/2 cup fresh, cooked; frozen, thawed; or drained, canned corn

1/2 cup drained rinsed black beans

2 scallions (including tender green tops), finely chopped

1/4 cup chopped cilantro leaves

**Jalapeño Cheese Quesadillas:**

Four 10-inch flour tortillas

2 cups shredded sharp Cheddar cheese

2 cups shredded Monterey Jack cheese

1/2 cup drained bottled sliced jalapeños

*To make the Southwest salsa:*
In a large bowl, stir together the salsa, corn, beans, scallions, and cilantro.

*To make the jalapeño cheese quesadillas:*
Preheat the oven to 450°F.

Lightly brush both sides of each tortilla with water. Place one tortilla on a baking sheet. Top half of the tortilla with 1/2 cup of the Cheddar cheese, 1/2 cup of the Monterey Jack cheese, and 2 tablespoons of the jalapeños. Fold the tortilla over to cover the filling. Repeat with the remaining ingredients.

Bake for 5 to 7 minutes, or until the quesadillas are lightly browned and the cheese is melted. Cut into wedges to serve. Serve with the Southwest salsa.

Makes 2 cups salsa; 4 servings.

# *What Was I Thinking When I Said, "Stop by Anytime,"* Major Grey's Marvelous Mango Chutney Cheese Spread

Here's a spread that has an intriguing medley of flavors that will have everyone returning to it again and again. It's best when allowed to come to room temperature. Leftovers make a delicious sandwich filling on a hearty whole grain bread such as pumpernickel.

1 package (8 ounces) cream cheese, softened

3 cups shredded sharp Cheddar cheese

Few drops of Tabasco pepper sauce

1 jar (10 ounces) Major Grey's mango chutney, chopped

5 strips of bacon, cooked until crisp, drained, and crumbled

6 scallions (including tender green tops), chopped

In a medium bowl, using a fork, stir together the cream cheese, 1 1/2 cups of the Cheddar cheese, and the pepper sauce until combined. Spread the mixture over an 8- to 10-inch serving dish, smoothing the surface evenly.

Spread the chutney over the surface. Sprinkle the chutney with the remaining 1 1/2 cups of Cheddar cheese, the bacon, and the scallions. Serve immediately with crackers or celery sticks. Cover and refrigerate any leftovers for up to two days.

Makes 8 to 10 servings.

# *Nothing Says Confidence Like a European Appetizer*
## Ooh la la Provençal Tapenade

This classic flavorful French spread is wonderful on crackers and slices of French bread. Its deep dark color looks great when served alongside Sassy Salsa Guacamole (page 63) and Red Pepper Dip/Spread (page 86). An alternative use is as an easy appetizer: scrub and cook small new potatoes until they are just tender. Cut the potatoes in half or into thick slices and spread a spoonful on top of each one.

1 can (6 ounces drained weight) pitted ripe olives, drained

1 can (2 ounces) anchovy fillets in olive oil, drained

2 tablespoons olive oil

1 tablespoon drained capers

1 tablespoon Dijon-style mustard

1 small garlic clove, coarsely chopped

Dash of Tabasco pepper sauce

Place all the ingredients in the container of a food processor fitted with a metal chopping blade. Process until the ingredients are combined, but still with a somewhat coarse texture, scraping down the side of the container with a rubber spatula if necessary. Scrape the spread into a small bowl. Serve immediately or cover and refrigerate to allow the flavors to blend. Can be served chilled or at room temperature.

Makes about 1 1/4 cups tapenade.

## *Since We're Only Having Brunch We Should Be Able to Eat Enough for the Two Other Meals We're Missing* Italian Sausage Mushroom Strata

Here's a recipe that is perfect for brunch. You assemble it the day before and then simply pop it into the oven to bake, enabling you to be a guest at your own party. To complete the menu, serve an assortment of quick breads and muffins along with a fruit salad made with seasonal fruits.

1 pound hot Italian sausage, casings removed

1 pound mushrooms, sliced

2 medium onions, sliced

1/2 cup sliced scallions

Enough Italian or French bread cut into 1-inch cubes to measure 9 cups

3 cups grated sharp Cheddar or other type of cheese

1 cup freshly grated Parmesan cheese

12 large eggs, lightly beaten

3 1/2 cups milk

3 tablespoons spicy brown mustard

1/4 teaspoon freshly ground black pepper

Lightly butter a 15-by-10-by-2 inch-(4-quart) baking dish.

In a large skillet, heat the sausage, mushrooms, and onions for about 20 minutes, or until the sausage is cooked through and the vegetables are tender. Drain off the fat. Stir in the scallions.

Arrange half of the bread cubes in the prepared baking dish. Spread half of the sausage-vegetable mixture over the bread cubes. Sprinkle half of the Cheddar cheese and half of the Parmesan cheese over the top. Repeat the layers.

In a large bowl, whisk together the eggs, milk, mustard, and pepper. Pour the egg mixture evenly over the strata. Cover and refrigerate the strata overnight.

Preheat the oven to 350°F. Bake for 50 to 60 minutes, or until the strata is puffed and golden and cooked through.

Makes 8 to 10 servings.

# *It's a Family Reunion and I Don't Know a Soul* Vegetarian Chili

Here's a fresh-tasting chili that you can easily assemble with your guests.  Ask for help chopping the vegetables and toppings and you can have it ready in a flash.  Serve ice cold beer as an accompaniment.  Use kitchen scissors to easily cut the canned tomatoes into pieces.  Just stick the point of the scissors right down into the open can and cut away until all the tomatoes are chopped.  For bean lovers, add an extra can of drained kidney beans. You can also use your favorite type of bean.

1 tablespoon vegetable oil

2 cups chopped onions

2 medium green bell peppers, seeded and chopped

3 medium garlic cloves, finely chopped

3 medium jalapeño peppers, seeded and finely chopped (leave the seeds in for a hotter chili)

3 tablespoons chili powder

1 teaspoon dried oregano leaves, crushed

1/2 teaspoon salt plus additional salt to taste

2 cans (35 ounces)  Italian-style plum tomatoes, chopped, with their juice

1 can (6 ounces) tomato paste

1 can (19 ounces) red kidney beans, drained

1 can (15 ounces) pinto beans, drained

1 can (15 ounces) garbanzo beans, drained

2 cups diced zucchini

Shredded sharp Cheddar cheese, sour cream, chopped onion or scallions, chopped tomatoes, or chopped olives for serving on top of the chili (optional)

In a large heavy saucepot, heat the oil over medium heat. Add the onions, peppers, garlic, and jalapeños. Cook for about 10 to 12 minutes, or until the vegetables are softened, stirring occasionally.

Stir in the chili powder, oregano, and salt. Add the tomatoes and their juice, tomato paste, and beans. Simmer for 25 minutes, stirring occasionally. Add the zucchini and cook for 5 to 10 minutes, continuing to stir occasionally. Season with salt. Ladle into bowls and serve with the toppings, if desired.

Makes about 15 cups chili; 10 to 12 servings.

# *You Never Know When You'll Meet the Man of Your Dreams So Be Sure to Bring a Good Dish* Marinated Vegetable Couscous Salad

Couscous is made from semolina which has been cracked. When cooked, it is similar to teeny tiny grains of rice. In this recipe, marinated vegetables are spooned into the center of a bed of couscous. This recipe makes a colorful side-dish salad.

1 box (10 ounces) couscous

1 can (13 3/4 ounces) chicken broth

4 cups broccoli flowerets

1 cup diagonally sliced carrots

3/4 cup vegetable oil

1/3 cup red wine vinegar

2 tablespoons freshly squeezed lemon juice

2 tablespoons Dijon-style mustard

1 tablespoon finely chopped fresh basil or 1 teaspoon dried basil leaves, crushed

1 medium garlic clove, cut in half

1/8 teaspoon freshly ground black pepper

1 (15-ounce) can garbanzo beans, drained

1 medium zucchini, diagonally sliced

1 medium yellow squash, diagonally sliced

1 medium red onion, coarsely chopped

1 medium red bell pepper, cored, seeded, and cut into 1-inch pieces

Place the couscous in a large heatproof bowl. In a medium-size saucepan, over high heat, bring the chicken broth to a boil. Pour the chicken broth over the couscous, stir, and cover. Let stand for 10 minutes so that the couscous absorbs the broth. Fluff the couscous with a fork.

Meanwhile, bring a large saucepot of water to a boil. Add the broccoli and carrots and cook for 1 minute. Rinse the broccoli and carrots under cold water and drain well.

In another large bowl, stir together the oil, vinegar, lemon juice, mustard, basil, garlic, and pepper. Add the broccoli, carrots, garbanzos, zucchini, yellow squash, red onion, and red pepper and toss to coat with the dressing.

Spread the couscous on a serving dish, building up the edges slightly. Top with the vegetables. Remove the garlic halves before serving.

Makes 6 servings.

## *She Gets a Bridal Shower and Twenty-Seven Gifts . . . I Get a Request to Bring Food* Brown and Wild Rice Salad with Carrots and Dried Cranberries

Serve this salad in a large bowl that is lined with green leaf lettuce. Turn the salad into the main event by adding 2 cups of bite-size pieces of cooked chicken.

3 1/4 cups water

1 1/2 teaspoons salt

1 cup uncooked brown rice

1/2 cup wild rice, rinsed and drained

1/3 cup vegetable oil

3 tablespoons red wine vinegar

1 tablespoon freshly squeezed lemon juice

1 tablespoon Dijon-style mustard

1 medium garlic clove, finely chopped

1/4 teaspoon Tabasco pepper sauce

1 cup dried cranberries

1 cup grated carrots

1/3 cup sliced scallions (including tender green tops)

1/2 cup coarsely broken toasted pecans (optional, see Note)

In a heavy large saucepan, bring the water and salt to a boil. Stir in the brown and wild rice and return the mixture to a boil. Reduce the heat, cover, and simmer for 50 to 60 minutes, or until the rice is tender and the water is completely absorbed.

Meanwhile, in a large bowl, stir together the oil, vinegar, lemon juice, mustard, garlic, and pepper sauce. Add the cooked rice and cranberries and let the mixture cool.

Stir in the carrots and scallions. Let the mixture stand at least 2 hours or refrigerate overnight to allow the flavors to blend. Before serving, let return to room temperature, adjust seasonings if necessary, and sprinkle the surface with the pecans, if desired.

Makes 6 to 8 servings.

Note: *To toast the nuts, place them in a single layer on a baking sheet and bake in a preheated 350°F. oven for 5 to 7 minutes, shaking the sheet a couple of times, until the nuts are lightly browned.*

## No, I Did NOT Buy This at a Deli and Throw Out the Container **Potato Green Bean Salad**

Bring this sturdy salad to your next picnic.  Make it the day before to allow the flavors to blend.

3 pounds small red potatoes, scrubbed and trimmed of blemishes

2 1/2 teaspoons salt

1 pound green beans, trimmed and cut into 1 1/2-inch pieces

1/4 cup olive oil

1/4 cup balsamic vinegar

2 tablespoons freshly squeezed lemon juice

2 tablespoons Dijon-style mustard

1 teaspoon finely chopped garlic

1/4 teaspoon freshly ground pepper

1/4 cup chopped fresh parsley (optional)

Place the potatoes in a large saucepot and add enough water to cover. Add 1 teaspoon of the salt. Cover the pot and bring the water to a boil. Reduce the heat and keep at a low boil for 30 to 40 minutes, or until the potatoes are tender when pierced with the tines of a fork. Thoroughly drain the potatoes. Cut the potatoes into 1 1/2-inch chunks.

Place the green beans in a large skillet. Add enough water to cover and 1 teaspoon of the salt. Cover and bring the mixture to a boil. Reduce the heat and simmer for 7 to 9 minutes, or until the beans are crisp-tender. Thoroughly drain.

Meanwhile, in a large bowl, stir together the oil, vinegar, lemon juice, mustard, garlic, remaining 1/2 teaspoon of salt, and pepper to make the dressing.

Add the warm cooked vegetables to the dressing and toss gently to combine. Cover and refrigerate, tossing gently occasionally. Right before serving, sprinkle with the chopped parsley, if desired.

Makes 6 to 8 servings.

## *Why Did I Volunteer to Bring Something* Party Pasta Salad

When it's time to create an easy dish to feed the masses, a pasta salad is hard to beat. This recipe idea could be scaled down to serve a single. Next time you cook pasta for dinner, make a little extra to use in a salad the next day. Make sure you cook the pasta in water that has been salted so it does not taste flat.

**16 ounces rotelle pasta (or another shape)**

**1 1/2 cups regular or reduced-calorie mayonnaise**

**1/3 cup red wine vinegar**

**3 tablespoons freshly squeezed lemon juice**

**1 tablespoon Dijon-style mustard**

**1 teaspoon salt**

**1/2 teaspoon dried basil leaves, crushed**

**1/2 teaspoon dried oregano leaves, crushed**

**1/4 teaspoon Tabasco pepper sauce**

**1 pound cooked shrimp, cut into 1/2-inch pieces (see Note)**

**1 medium red bell pepper, seeded and chopped**

**1 medium tomato, chopped**

**1 cup chopped pitted ripe olives**

**1/2 cup chopped fresh parsley**

Cook the pasta according to the package directions in lightly salted water. Rinse with cold water and drain thoroughly.

Meanwhile, in a large bowl, stir together the mayonnaise, vinegar, lemon juice, mustard, salt, basil, oregano, and Tabasco. Add the pasta, shrimp, pepper, tomato, olives, and parsley and toss gently to coat the ingredients with the dressing. Cover and refrigerate at least one hour. Toss the salad gently, taste, and adjust the seasonings.

Makes about 8 servings.

Note: *Other types of cooked seafood, chicken, or turkey could be used in place of the shrimp. For instance, substitute 2 cans (6 ounces) tuna or 1 can (12 ounces) tuna, drained and flaked, for the shrimp. Cooked, canned, or frozen crabmeat is also delicious.*

## *Keep Them Eating and They Won't Have Time to Look in My Bathroom Cabinets*
# Apple Cranberry Crisp

This is wonderful topped with a big scoop of vanilla ice cream or sweetened cream. You can trim off the peels of the apples if you'd like, but it is also delicious with the peels. Try other fruits baked underneath this flavorful topping mixture.

**4 medium tart apples (such as Granny Smith), cored and sliced**

**1 cup fresh or thawed frozen cranberries**

**2/3 cup firmly packed brown sugar**

**1/2 cup all-purpose flour**

**1/2 cup uncooked old-fashioned rolled oats**

**1/3 cup unsalted butter, softened**

**3/4 teaspoon ground cinnamon**

**1/4 teaspoon ground ginger**

Preheat the oven to 375°F. Lightly butter the bottom and sides of an 8- or 9-inch square baking pan.

Toss the apple slices and cranberries together in the prepared pan.

In a medium bowl, stir together the brown sugar, flour, oats, butter, cinnamon, and ginger and sprinkle the mixture over the fruit. Bake for 25 to 30 minutes, or until the topping is lightly browned and the fruits are tender. It is best served warm.

Makes 6 servings.

## *I'll Need at Least Three Hours to Prepare My Casual, Carefree Look, so I'd Better Get Started* Make-Ahead Ziti Bake

Here's a hearty Italian-style dish that you can make ahead of time. Offer balsamic vinegar and extra-virgin olive oil as accompaniments for dipping hearty whole grain bread into. Serve with a tossed salad to fill out the meal.

16 ounces ziti

2 tablespoons olive oil

2 cups chopped onions

4 medium garlic cloves, finely chopped

1 tablespoon dried basil leaves, crushed

1/2 teaspoon crushed red pepper flakes

1/4 teaspoon dried oregano leaves, crushed

3 cans (28 ounces) Italian-style plum tomatoes, drained and chopped

1 can (8 ounces) tomato sauce

1/4 cup tomato paste

1 pound mozzarella cheese, shredded

1 cup freshly grated Parmesan cheese

HOSTESS WITH THE MOSTEST

PANIC  INSECURITY

ANXIETY  GUILT

Cook the pasta according to the package directions and drain thoroughly.

In a large heavy saucepan, heat the oil over medium heat. Add the onions, garlic, basil, red pepper flakes, and oregano. Cook for about 5 to 7 minutes, or until the vegetables are softened, stirring occasionally.

Stir in the chopped tomatoes, tomato sauce, and tomato paste. Simmer, uncovered, for 30 to 40 minutes, or until the mixture has thickened slightly, stirring occasionally.

Preheat the oven to 350°F.

In a large bowl combine the cooked pasta, tomato sauce, half of the mozzarella cheese, and the Parmesan cheese. Place the mixture in a 13 by 9 by 2 inch (3-quart) baking dish. Cover the dish with aluminum foil and bake for 20 minutes. Uncover and sprinkle the surface evenly with the remaining mozzarella cheese. Bake for 10 minutes longer, or until the cheese is melted.

Makes 8 to 10 servings.

Note: *The ziti can be prepared up to 2 days ahead of time. Before sprinkling the mozzarella cheese on top, cover and refrigerate the ziti mixture. When ready to serve, bake the ziti mixture, covered, for 40 to 50 minutes, or until the mixture is heated through. Sprinkle the surface evenly with the remaining mozzarella cheese and bake for 10 minutes longer.*

## *Oh No, He Invited His Mother*
# Fillet of Beef with Horseradish Sauce

If you start with one of the most tender cuts of meat (at a price, of course), it's difficult to mess it up. Fillet of beef is delicious served hot or at room temperature, so the pressure is off to get everything done at the same time. It is great served as part of a buffet. Allow about 1/2 pound of raw fillet per person.

**Fillet of Beef:**

1 (at least 6-pound) fillet of beef

6 strips of bacon

Salt and freshly ground black pepper to taste

**Horseradish Sauce:**

1/2 cup heavy (whipping) cream, chilled

1/2 cup prepared horse-radish, drained

1/2 cup mayonnaise

2 tablespoons Dijon-style mustard

1/4 teaspoon Tabasco pepper sauce

*To make the fillet of beef:*
With a sharp, pointed knife, trim the fat and thin fibrous covering from the fillet. Tuck the thin tail end under the fillet and secure it with a string. Let the fillet stand at room temperature for about 1 hour before cooking.

Preheat the oven to 500°F. Place the fillet on a rack in a roasting pan and lay the strips of bacon over the meat. Reduce the heat immediately to 400°F. and bake for about 30 minutes. The fillet is rare when the internal temperature is 120 to 125°F. on a meat thermometer. For medium rare, cook to 130 to 140°F. For medium, cook to 145 to 150°F. For well done, cook to 155 to 165°F. Remove the bacon and continue cooking the bacon longer, if desired, to serve it alongside the fillet. Cut the meat into 1/2-to-3/4-inch-thick slices.

*To make the horseradish sauce:*
In a chilled medium bowl, using a handheld electric mixer with chilled beaters set at medium-high speed, beat the cream until peaks just start to form.

In large bowl, stir together the horseradish, mayonnaise, mustard, and pepper sauce. Using a rubber spatula, gently fold one third of the whipped cream into the horseradish mixture to lighten it. Fold in the remaining whipped cream just until combined. Serve with the sliced fillet and bacon.

Makes at least 18 servings (if you allow about 1/3 pound of cooked meat per person).

## *I'm Sure Someone Was Born Today*
# Chocolate Chip Birthday Cake

This delicious two-layer cake could give you a reputation as baker extraordinare. It's easy and much more "natural" than making a cake mix or serving a store-bought cake. This dense white cake is chock full of chocolate chips and then the whole shebang is coated with a rich chocolatey frosting.

**Cake:**

1 1/2 cups semisweet chocolate chips

2 3/4 cups all-purpose flour, divided

2 teaspoons baking powder

1/2 teaspoon salt

1 cup (2 sticks) unsalted butter or margarine, softened

1 3/4 cups granulated sugar

4 large eggs, at room temperature

2 teaspoons vanilla extract

1 1/3 cups milk, at room temperature

**Chocolate Frosting:**

1 box (16 ounces) chocolate-flavored confectioners' sugar

1/2 cup (1 stick) butter or margarine, softened

1/3 cup milk

1 teaspoon vanilla extract

*To make the cake:*
Preheat the oven to 350°F.  Lightly butter two 9-inch round cake pans.  Dust the pans with flour and lightly tap them to shake out the excess flour.

In a medium bowl, stir together the chocolate chips and 2 tablespoons of the flour until combined. (This will prevent the chocolate chips from settling to the bottom.)

In a large bowl, stir together the remaining flour, baking powder, and salt.

In another large bowl with an electric mixer set on high speed, beat the butter and sugar for about 2 minutes until well blended.  One at a time, beat in the eggs, beating well after each addition.  Beat in the vanilla extract.

With the mixer set on low speed, in three additions each, alternately beat in the flour mixture and the milk, scraping the side of the bowl as necessary.  Beat until the ingredients are just incorporated.  Using a wooden spoon, stir in the chocolate chips.

Divide the batter evenly between the prepared pans and smooth the surface.  (There will about 3 cups of batter in each pan.)  Bake for 30 to 35 minutes, or until a toothpick inserted into the center of each cake layer comes out clean.  Cool the cakes in the pans set on a wire rack for 15 minutes.  Carefully remove the cakes from the pans and cool completely on the wire rack.

Makes 12 to 14 servings.

*To make the chocolate frosting:*
In a large bowl, with an electric mixer set on high speed, beat the confectioners' sugar, butter, milk, and vanilla until smooth, adding a small amount of milk if necessary to achieve a frosting of spreading consistency.

Place one cake layer on a serving platter.  Spread with about 3/4 cup of frosting.  Place the second cake layer on top.  Frost the side and then the top of the cake.

Remove the cakes [illegible]

[illegible] the [illegible] to 300°F. [illegible] together [illegible] sugar [illegible] cake [illegible] but the [illegible] with [illegible] an [illegible] or [illegible] it slides off the [illegible] Now [illegible]

[illegible] the chocolate [illegible] of the [illegible] all [illegible] will [illegible] the chocolate [illegible] the [illegible]

In a large bowl, sift together the remaining flour, baking powder, and salt.

In another large bowl, with an electric mixer set on high speed, beat the butter and sugar for about 2 minutes until well blended. [illegible] the [illegible] in the [illegible] beat [illegible] well after each addition. Beat in the vanilla extract.

With the mixer set on low speed, add the dry ingredients [illegible] alternately with the milk mixture, and the milk, scraping the side of the bowl as necessary. Then with the [illegible] until [illegible] blended. Using a wooden spoon, stir in the chocolate [illegible]

[illegible] the batter evenly between the prepared pans and smooth the surface. Bake until about [illegible] comes out clean, 30 to 35 minutes. [illegible] a toothpick inserted into the [illegible] of [illegible] comes out clean. [illegible] the [illegible] in the pans on a wire rack for 10 minutes. Carefully remove the cakes from the pans and cool completely on the wire rack.

Makes 12 to 14 servings.

[illegible] Chocolate Frosting
In a large bowl, with an electric mixer set on high speed, beat the confectioners' sugar, butter, milk, [illegible] vanilla until [illegible] smooth [illegible]. If necessary, [illegible] of [illegible] frosting.

Place one cake layer on a serving plate. [illegible] over the top. Place the second cake layer on top. Frost the sides and then the top of the cake.

# Consolation Food

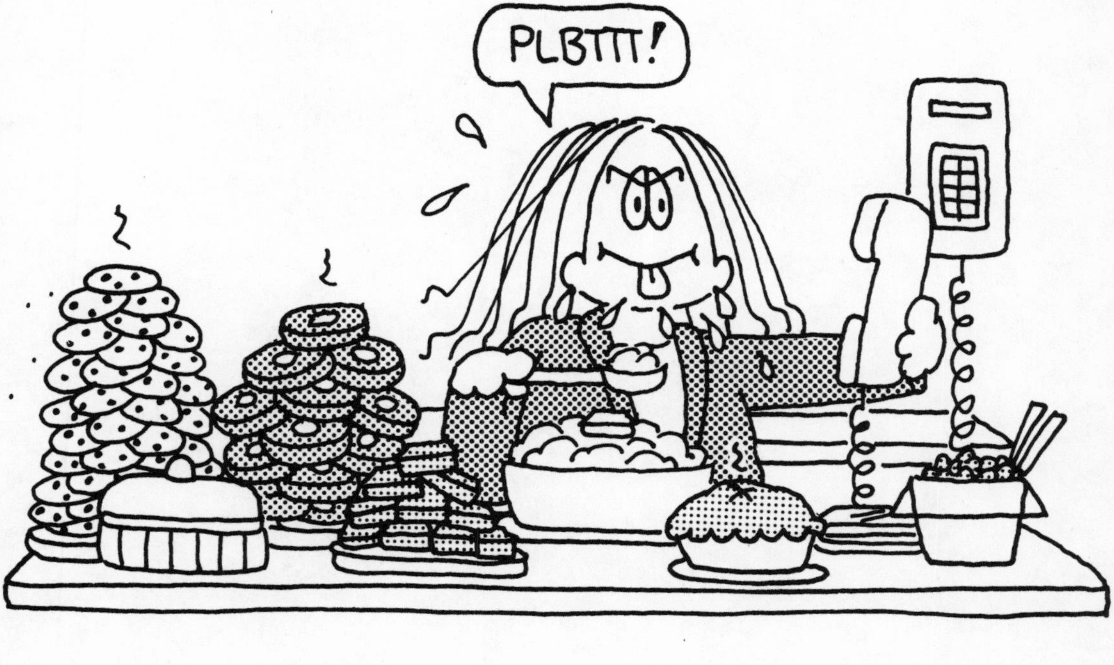
PLBTTT!

# Consolation Food

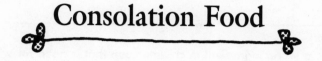

I've never met a man who understood me as well as a chocolate chip cookie, and in a way, I hope I never do.

When I'm miserable, I don't want empathetic dialogue. I want food. Food like Mom used to make for me. Food like Mom would still make for me if I were willing to invite her over, tell her everything, and listen to her advice.

I want to act like a five-year-old, sound like a five-year-old, and eat like a five-year-old. I want food that hugs me inside and out. Food that says, "Plbttt!!" to the rest of the world. Food that instantly re-creates that beautiful, perfect time of life when I believed with all my heart that the entire universe revolved around me.

I want food that restores my confidence, my sense of justice, my equilibrium, my perspective, and my sense of humor.

You just can't stay that bummed for that long with a spoonful of really, really good mashed potatoes in your mouth.

## *The Proposal Is Due; I Lost the File; I'm Staying Home* Chicken Noodle Soup

**There seems to be a secret ingredient in chicken soup that is good for whatever ails you.**

1 tablespoon olive oil

1 cup chopped onion

1 cup chopped celery

1 medium garlic clove, finely chopped

4 cups chicken broth or stock

1 can (16 ounces) whole tomatoes, undrained and cut up

1 package (10 ounces) frozen mixed vegetables

1 teaspoon dried basil leaves, crushed

1 medium bay leaf

1 cup medium egg noodles

2 cups bite-size pieces of cooked chicken

Salt and pepper to taste

In a large saucepot, heat the oil over medium heat. Add the onion, celery, and garlic and cook, stirring frequently, for 5 to 7 minutes, or until the vegetables are tender.

Add the chicken broth, tomatoes and juice, vegetables, basil, and bay leaf. Bring the mixture to a boil. Stir in the noodles and cook for 7 minutes longer. Add the chicken and continue cooking until the mixture is heated through. Remove the bay leaf before serving. Season with salt and pepper. Serve in warmed mugs or bowls.

Makes about 9 cups soup; 4 to 6 servings.

## *My Favorite Show Was Canceled and Replaced by Superbowl Highlights* Grilled Cheese Sandwich

Of course, for ultimate comfort, have one of these soul-satisfying sandwiches with a mug of tomato soup. While the classic combo is American cheese and white bread, try other varieties of cheese. For instance, Brie is a sophisticated filling with hearty whole grain bread. Add a slice of ham if you like. If your butter is straight from the fridge, soften it by putting it in a small microwave-safe dish in the microwave oven. Put the oven on the defrost setting and defrost for 20 to 30 seconds until the butter is of spreading consistency.

2 to 3 teaspoons butter, softened

2 slices of bread

2 to 3 slices of cheese

Spread half of the butter on one side of each piece of bread. Place the cheese in between the bread slices, with the buttered sides facing out. Heat a nonstick skillet over medium-high heat. Place the sandwich in the pan and cook for 2 to 3 minutes on each side, or until lightly browned.

Makes 1 serving.

BAD HAIR
BAD FACE
BAD BODY
AND
BAD BRAIN
DAY

# *The Guy I Dumped in Junior High Just Purchased Asia* **Macaroni and Cheese**

**If you like macaroni and cheese that is a little soupier, add an extra 1/4 cup of milk.**

1 package (8 ounces) elbow macaroni

1 tablespoon butter

1 tablespoon all-purpose flour

1/4 teaspoon dry mustard

Dash of ground pepper

1 1/2 cups milk

8 ounces pasteurized processed cheese spread (such as Velveeta), cut into 1/2-inch pieces

Preheat the oven to 350°F. Cook the macaroni according to the package directions and drain thoroughly.

In a large saucepan, melt the butter over medium heat. Stir in the flour, mustard, and pepper and cook, stirring constantly until combined. Gradually stir in the milk and continue to cook, stirring frequently, until the mixture is hot. Add the cheese spread and continue cooking and stirring until the cheese spread has melted. Remove the pan from the heat and stir in the macaroni just until combined. Scrape the mixture into an 1 1/2-quart baking dish. Bake for 25 minutes, or until bubbly.

Makes 4 servings.

## *My Credit Card Bill Just Arrived*
# Tuna Noodle Casserole

**When it comes to comfort, sometimes nothing else will do than this easy tried-and-true classic. If your guy is a classic kind of guy, you might want to file this under the Romance chapter!**

**3 cups medium noodles (about 4 ounces) or 1 cup elbow macaroni (3 1/2 ounces)**

**1 tablespoon butter**

**1/2 cup chopped onion**

**1 can (10 3/4 ounces) condensed cream of mushroom soup**

**3/4 cup milk**

**1 can (about 7 ounces) tuna, drained and flaked**

**1 cup frozen peas or frozen peas and carrots**

**1/2 cup crushed potato chips (optional)**

Preheat the oven to 400°F. Cook the noodles or macaroni according to the package directions and drain thoroughly.

In a large saucepan, melt the butter over medium heat. Add the onion and cook, stirring frequently, for 4 to 6 minutes, or until the onion is tender.

Stir in the soup, milk, tuna, and vegetables just until mixed. Stir in the noodles just until combined. Scrape the mixture into a 1 1/2-quart baking dish. Bake for 20 minutes, or until heated through. If desired, sprinkle with the crushed potato chips and bake 5 minutes longer.

Makes 4 servings.

## *Does Everyone Drive Like an Idiot* Chicken Pot Pie

**Frozen puff pastry makes a delectable topping for this homey chicken pot pie.**

**2 tablespoons butter**

**1 cup chopped onion**

**1/3 cup all-purpose flour**

**1 teaspoon fresh marjoram leaves, chopped or 1/2 teaspoon dried marjoram leaves, crushed**

**1 1/2 cups milk**

**1 1/2 cups chicken broth or stock**

**3 cups bite-size pieces of cooked chicken**

**1 package (10 ounces) frozen peas and carrots**

**1/4 cup chopped fresh parsley**

**Salt and ground white pepper to taste**

**1/2 package (17 1/4 ounces) frozen puff pastry sheets (1 sheet), thawed according to package directions**

**1 egg yolk mixed with 1 teaspoon water (for the egg wash)**

Preheat the oven to 400°F.

In a large saucepot, melt the butter over medium heat. Add the onion and cook, stirring frequently, for 4 to 6 minutes, or until the onion is tender. Stir in the flour and marjoram. Add the milk and broth and continue cooking, stirring constantly, for about 5 minutes, or until the sauce thickens slightly. Stir in the chicken, peas and carrots, and parsley. Season with salt and pepper and continue cooking until the mixture is hot. Spoon the chicken mixture into a 1 1/2-quart baking dish.

Place the pastry loosely over the filling in the baking dish. With kitchen shears, trim the edge of the pastry, leaving a 1-inch overhang. Brush the top surface of the pastry with the egg wash. Bake for 15 to 20 minutes, or until the pastry is golden brown. (To eliminate spills onto the bottom of your oven: position one oven rack in the center of the oven. Position another rack underneath and place a baking sheet on the lower rack to catch any drips.)

Makes 4 servings.

# *I Want to Go Home But I Don't Want to Live There* Meatloaf

Here's a flavorful meatloaf that is chock full of mushrooms! Make sure to save some for a leftover meatloaf sandwich or two.

**2 teaspoons vegetable oil**

**1 1/2 cups sliced mushrooms**

**1 medium onion, chopped**

**1 1/2 pounds ground beef**

**3/4 cup Italian-seasoned dry bread crumbs**

**2 large eggs**

**2 tablespoons Dijon-style mustard**

**1/4 teaspoon freshly ground black pepper**

**1 teaspoon prepared horseradish**

Preheat the oven to 350°F. In a large skillet, heat the oil over medium heat. Add the mushrooms and onion and cook, stirring occasionally, for 8 to 10 minutes, or until the vegetables are softened. Remove the pan from the heat.

In a large bowl, using your hands or a wooden spoon, mix the cooked vegetables and the remaining ingredients until well combined.

Spoon the mixture into a 9-by-5-by-3-inch ovenproof glass loaf pan and smooth the surface. Bake for 1 hour, or until cooked through and no longer pink in the center. Loosen the loaf from the pan and drain off the drippings. Invert the meatloaf onto a warmed serving platter. Let stand for 5 minutes before cutting into slices to serve.

Makes 6 servings.

## *Who Needs Him Anyway*
## Mashed Potatoes

When it comes to comfort, there is nothing like a big bowl of mashed potatoes to soothe the soul.  While many people like their mashed potatoes left unadulterated, try stirring in a small amount of one or more of the following to add extra interest:  grated Parmesan, Cheddar, or another type of cheese; chopped scallions or red onions; chopped, drained, oil-packed sun-dried tomatoes; or chopped raw or cooked garlic.  Use a potato masher instead of an electric mixer to work out a lot of anxiety.

**6 medium potatoes, scrubbed**

**1 teaspoon salt plus additional salt to taste**

**1/4 cup butter, softened**

**Ground white pepper to taste**

**1/4 to 1/2 cup hot milk**

In a large saucepot, combine the potatoes, enough water to cover, and 1 teaspoon of the salt.  Cover the pot and bring the mixture to a slow boil and cook for 30 to 35 minutes, or until the potatoes are tender.  Drain and peel the potatoes.  (You can trim off the blemishes and leave on all or some of the skin if you like for a little extra texture.)  Return the potatoes to the pan.

Using a handheld electric mixer or a potato masher, beat the potatoes with the butter until combined.  Season with salt and pepper.  Gradually add 1/4 cup of the hot milk and beat. Beat in more milk if necessary to create potatoes that are light and fluffy.  Do not overbeat. Serve immediately or scrape the potatoes into a buttered casserole and keep warm in a 250°F. oven.

Makes about 6 cups mashed potatoes; 4 to 6 servings.

## *My Make-Over Took Seven Hours* Hot Fudge Sauce

This multi-purpose sauce can be poured over whatever you want — cake, ice cream, brownie sundaes, etc. If you like, you can add a tablespoon of your favorite liqueur (such as cognac, Chambord, or Grand Marnier) along with the vanilla. Basically it is a ganache (a mixture of heavy cream and chocolate). If you freeze the mixture, it can then be shaped into small (about 1 to 2 teaspoons) balls to form the base for truffles. After you form the balls, roll them into finely chopped nuts. Freeze the truffles for up to one month. Let thaw slightly before serving.

2/3 cup heavy (whipping) cream

1 1/2 teaspoons unsalted butter

A few grains of salt

3/4 teaspoon instant espresso or coffee powder

6 ounces bittersweet chocolate, finely chopped

1 teaspoon vanilla extract

In a heavy, small saucepan, combine the cream, butter, and salt. Slowly bring the mixture to a gentle boil over medium-low heat. Remove the pan from the heat. Stir in the espresso powder. Whisk in the chocolate until smooth. Stir in the vanilla.

Makes about 1 1/2 cups sauce.

## *I Really, Really, Really Deserve a Raise* **Buttermilk Doughnuts**

Homemade doughnuts are a little more work than driving to the local doughnut shop. However, once you get the hang of them, you'll probably want to make them over and over again. Plus when you make them at home, you don't have to put on your makeup for the doughnut man (or order an embarrassingly large number of doughnuts for yourself). To transfer the doughnuts for frying without stretching them out of shape, dip a metal pancake turner into the hot oil. Pick up the doughnuts and they will slide right off! Try these doughnuts served with hot or cold apple cider after an invigorating fall walk.

3 1/4 cups all-purpose flour

2 teaspoons baking powder

1 teaspoon baking soda

1 teaspoon ground cinnamon

1/2 teaspoon ground ginger

1/2 teaspoon salt

2 large eggs

1 cup granulated sugar plus extra for coating (optional)

2/3 cup buttermilk

1/4 cup unsalted butter, melted

1 1/2 teaspoons vanilla extract

Vegetable oil for deep-fat frying

Confectioners' sugar, cinnamon sugar, or Chocolate Glaze (recipe follows) for coating (optional)

WAAH!

DESSERT TIME!

In a large bowl, sift together the flour, baking powder, baking soda, cinnamon, ginger, and salt.

In another large bowl, using a handheld electric mixer set at medium-high speed, beat the eggs and granulated sugar until combined. In a small bowl, stir together the buttermilk, butter, and vanilla until combined. Beat this mixture into the egg mixture. With the mixer set on low speed, add the flour mixture and beat just until smooth. Cover the dough and refrigerate it for about 1 hour.

In a deep-fat fryer or a heavy saucepot, heat the oil to 375°F.

While the oil is heating, cut out the doughnuts. On a well-floured work surface, with a floured rolling pin or floured hands, roll or pat the dough out so it is about 1/2 inch thick. With a floured doughnut cutter, cut out the doughnuts and doughnut holes. Gather the scraps together and reroll and cut out the doughnuts and holes until all the dough is used.

Add the doughnuts, three at a time, and cook for about 30 to 60 seconds on each side, or until golden, turning once with a slotted spoon. Lift the doughnuts from the hot oil with the slotted spoon and drain the doughnuts on several layers of paper towels. Repeat with the remaining doughnuts and doughnut holes (cooking about eight of the holes together at a time). Serve them as is, or shake them in a bag with granulated, confectioners', or cinnamon sugar, or dip or drizzle the tops with Chocolate Glaze, if desired.

Makes about 16 doughnuts.

# Chocolate Glaze

Great for dunking Buttermilk Doughnuts (page 124) into, this also makes a decadent glaze or drizzle for cakes.  Sprinkle a few chopped nuts, colored sprinkles, or toasted coconut on top of the glaze for extra decadence.

**4 ounces semisweet chocolate**

**3 tablespoons unsalted butter**

**1/2 teaspoon vanilla extract**

**1 1/2 cups sifted confectioners' sugar**

**2 to 4 tablespoons hot water**

In a large microwave-safe bowl, heat the chocolate and butter in a microwave oven on high for 1 to 3 minutes, stirring halfway through cooking, until the chocolate is melted (or use a double boiler over hot, not simmering, water).  Whisk in the vanilla.  Whisk in the confectioners' sugar.  Whisk in enough hot water to make the glaze of the right consistency for either dunking doughnuts or drizzling over cakes.

Makes about 1 1/2 cups glaze.

# I've Been Waiting for His "I'll Call You" for the Last Twelve Days **Colossal Chocolate Chip Peanut Butter Cookies**

**If you only want to eat one cookie, this is the one to go for. Each cookie measures about 5 inches across. They freeze well.**

2 cups all-purpose flour

2 cups uncooked old-fash-
ioned rolled oats

1 teaspoon baking powder

1 teaspoon baking soda

1/2 teaspoon salt

1 cup (2 sticks) unsalted butter, softened

1 cup crunchy peanut butter

2 cups firmly packed brown
sugar

2 large eggs, at room
temperature

1 tablespoon vanilla extract

2 cups semisweet chocolate
chips

In a large bowl, stir together the flour, oats, baking powder, baking soda, and salt. In another large bowl, using a wooden spoon, cream together the butter, peanut butter, and sugar. One at a time, add the eggs, stirring well after each addition. Stir in the vanilla. Gradually stir in the flour mixture until combined. Stir in the chocolate chips. Cover and refrigerate the dough for at least 2 hours or overnight.

Preheat the oven to 300°F. Position one oven rack in the top one third of the oven and the other oven rack in the bottom third of the oven. Using a 1/2-cup measuring cup, drop the dough by cupfuls onto baking sheets, putting only 5 mounds on each large baking sheet so there is about 3 inches in between cookies. Flatten each mound slightly. Bake the cookies for 40 to 45 minutes, switching the positions of the baking sheets halfway through baking, until the cookies are lightly golden. Remove the baking sheets to wire racks and cool for 5 minutes. Using a metal spatula, transfer the cookies to wire racks and cool completely. Repeat until all the dough is used. When cool, store the cookies in an airtight container for up to 2 weeks.

These cookies freeze well for up to 3 months.

Makes about 14 jumbo cookies.

## *I Swear I'll Never Buy Anything Else*
# Chocolate Chip Cookies (or Dough)

This cookie dough freezes well. For future snacking, package the dough into portion-controlled servings and store it in the freezer for up to 3 months.

2 1/4 cups all-purpose flour

3/4 teaspoon baking powder

1/4 teaspoon salt

1 cup (2 sticks) unsalted butter, softened

3/4 cup firmly packed dark brown sugar

1/2 cup granulated sugar

2 large eggs, at room temperature

2 teaspoons vanilla extract

2 cups semisweet chocolate chips

1 cup chopped walnuts or pecans

In a large bowl, stir together the flour, baking powder, and salt. In another bowl, using a wooden spoon, cream together the butter and sugars. One at a time, add the eggs, stirring well after each addition. Stir in the vanilla. Gradually stir in the flour mixture until combined. Stir in the chocolate chips and nuts. Eat the dough. (See Note below.)

Makes about 5 cups dough.

*Chocolate Chip Cookie Variation:*
Cover and refrigerate the dough (any that is left over) for at least 2 hours or overnight.

Preheat the oven to 350°F. Drop the dough by rounded tablespoonfuls onto an ungreased baking sheet, leaving 2 inches between the dough mounds. Bake for 10 to 13 minutes, or until the cookies are lightly browned. Remove the baking sheet to a wire rack and cool for 5 minutes. Using a metal spatula, transfer the cookies to wire racks and cool completely. Repeat until all the dough is used. When cool, store the cookies in an airtight container for up to 2 weeks.

These cookies freeze well for up to 3 months.

If all the dough turns into cookies, you should get about 50 cookies.

Note: *There is some concern about getting salmonella from eating raw eggs. While the American Egg Board has not learned of any cases of salmonella resulting from eating uncooked cookie dough, if you are concerned, use a pasteurized egg product available in the refrigerated and freezer sections of the grocery store.*

# *I Want Comfort and I Want It Now* **Fast Fudge**

**This easy fudge recipe is made with cream cheese as its base so there is no need to hassle with a candy thermometer.**

**1 package (8 ounces) cream cheese, softened**

**8 ounces semisweet choco- late, melted and cooled**

**1 teaspoon vanilla extract**

**1 cup chopped walnuts or pecans**

Lightly coat an 8-inch-square pan with nonstick vegetable cooking spray.

In a large bowl, using a handheld electric mixer, beat the cream cheese just until it is smooth. Beat in the melted chocolate and vanilla. Using a wooden spoon, stir in the nuts.

Scrape the batter into the prepared pan and spread even- ly. Cover and refrigerate the fudge until it is firm. Cut into 1-inch squares. Store in an airtight container in the refrig- erator for up to 2 weeks.

Makes about 64 candies.

# *I Think I'm Going Insane*
# **Peanut Butter Squares**

Peanuts and chocolate are one of America's favorite flavor combinations. In fact, the leading candy bars sold in the United States (Snickers, Reese's Peanut Butter Cups, and Peanut M & M's) all contain these two ingredients. This recipe is similar to a Reese's Peanut Butter Cup — only in a jumbo 8-inch-square size!

**3 ounces white chocolate, broken into pieces**

**3/4 cup crunchy peanut butter**

**2/3 cup confectioners' sugar**

**1 tablespoon vanilla extract**

**3 ounces bittersweet chocolate, broken into pieces**

Lightly spray an 8-inch-square baking pan with vegetable cooking spray.

In a microwave-safe bowl, heat the white chocolate on high for 1 to 2 minutes, stirring halfway through cooking, until the chocolate is melted (or use a double boiler over hot, not simmering, water). Stir in the peanut butter, confectioners' sugar, and vanilla until combined. Scrape the mixture into the prepared pan and spread it into an even layer.

In a microwave-safe bowl, heat the bittersweet chocolate on high for 1 to 2 minutes, stirring halfway through cooking, until the chocolate is melted (or use a double boiler over hot, not simmering, water). Quickly pour the chocolate over the peanut butter and spread it evenly over the surface. Refrigerate until set. Cut into 1-inch squares. (If it is difficult to make even cuts through the chocolate, let the pan stand at room temperature before cutting into squares.)

Makes about 64 candies.

## *My Hair Dryer Just Broke and I Can't Leave the House* **Ice Cream Pie**

**The base of this pie is basically a jumbo chocolate chip cookie. Topped with ice cream, it is a decadent combination of two consolation foods.**

1 1/4 cups all-purpose flour

1/2 teaspoon baking powder

1/4 teaspoon salt

1/2 cup (1 stick) unsalted butter, softened

1/2 cup firmly packed brown sugar

1/4 cup granulated sugar

1 large egg, at room temperature

1 teaspoon vanilla extract

1 cup semisweet chocolate chips

5 cups vanilla ice cream or any other flavor

Sweetened whipped cream, chocolate shavings, or Hot Fudge Sauce (page 123) for topping (optional)

Preheat the oven to 375°F. Generously butter a 9-inch oven proof pie plate.

In a large bowl, stir together the flour, baking powder, and salt. In another bowl, using a wooden spoon, cream together the butter and sugars. Add the egg, stirring well. Stir in the vanilla. Gradually stir in the flour mixture until combined. Stir in the chocolate chips.

Scrape the batter into the prepared pie plate and smooth the surface evenly. Bake for 25 to 30 minutes, or until it is lightly golden and a toothpick inserted into the center comes out clean. Set on a wire rack and cool the cookie crust in the plate.

When the crust is completely cooled, let the ice cream stand at room temperature for 10 to 15 minutes, or until it is softened slightly. Mound the ice cream on top of the crust and smooth the surface. Cover the pie loosely with plastic wrap and freeze at least 4 hours, or until the ice cream is firm enough to cut into wedges. Top the pie with sweetened whipped cream, chocolate shavings, or Hot Fudge Sauce, if desired.

Makes 8 servings.

# *I'm Turning into My Mother Anyway,* *So Why Not Eat Some* Chocolate Pudding

When you are looking for an intense chocolate experience and the satisfaction of smooth and creamy pudding, here's the recipe to go for. Unsweetened chocolate adds extra chocolate flavor to the smooth and delicious bittersweet chocolate that is used in the pudding.

1 cup granulated sugar

1/3 cup cornstarch

Pinch of salt

3 large egg yolks, lightly beaten

4 cups whole milk

6 ounces bittersweet chocolate, finely chopped

2 ounces unsweetened chocolate, finely chopped

2 teaspoons vanilla extract

In a large heavy saucepan, stir together the sugar, cornstarch, and salt. Gradually whisk in the egg yolks until they are combined. Gradually whisk in the milk.

Cook the mixture over medium heat, stirring constantly with a whisk, for about 10 minutes, or until the mixture thickens and comes to a boil. Remove the pan from the heat and whisk in the chocolates and vanilla, whisking until smooth. Quickly pour the mixture through a strainer into a bowl. Serve at once or cover the surface of the pudding with a piece of plastic wrap to prevent a "skin" from forming. Refrigerate any leftover pudding.

Makes about 6 cups pudding; servings vary according to the comfort needs of the consumer.

# Index

# Index

# Index

# Metric Conversions

## WEIGHTS

| Ounces and Pounds | Metrics |
|---|---|
| 1/4 ounce | 7 grams |
| 1/3 ounce | 10 g |
| 1/2 ounce | 14 g |
| 1 ounce | 28 g |
| 1 1/3 ounces | 42 g |
| 1 3/4 ounces | 50 g |
| 2 ounces | 57 g |
| 3 ounces | 85 g |
| 3 1/2 ounces | 100 g |
| 4 ounces (1/4 pound) | 114 g |
| 6 ounces ± | 70 g |
| 8 ounces (1/2 pound) | 227 g |
| 9 ounces | 250 g |
| 16 ounces (1 pound) | 464 g |

## TEMPERATURES

| °F (Fahrenheit) | | °C (Centigrade or Celcius) |
|---|---|---|
| 32 | (water freezes) | 0 |
| 200 | | 95 |
| 212 | (water boils) | 100 |
| 250 | | 120 |
| 275 | | 135 |
| 300 | (slow oven) | 150 |
| 325 | | 160 |
| 350 | (moderate oven) | 175 |
| 375 | | 190 |
| 400 | (hot oven) | 205 |
| 425 | | 220 |
| 450 | (very hot oven) | 232 |
| 475 | | 245 |
| 500 | (extremely hot oven) | 260 |

## LIQUID MEASURES

tsp.=teaspoon   Tbs.=tablespoon

| Spoons and Cups | Metrics |
|---|---|
| 1/4 tsp. | 1.23 milliliters |
| 1/2 tsp. | 2.5 mm |
| 3/4 tsp. | 3.7 mm |
| 1 tsp. | 5 mm |
| 1 desert spoon | 10 mm |
| 1 Tbs.(3 tsp.) | 15 mm |
| 2 Tbs. (1 ounce) | 30 mm |
| 1/4 cup | 60 mm |
| 1/3 cup | 80 mm |
| 1/2 cup | 120 mm |
| 2/3 cup | 160 mm |
| 3/4 cup | 180 mm |
| 1 cup | 240 mm |
| 2 cups (1 pint) | 480 mm |
| 3 cups | 720 mm |
| 4 cups (1 quart) | ± liter |
| 4 quarts (1 gallon) | 3 3/4 liters |

## LENGTH

| U.S. Measurements | | Metrics | |
|---|---|---|---|
| 1/8 | inch | 3 | mm |
| 1/4 | inch | 6 | mm |
| 3/8 | inch | 1 | cm |
| 1/2 | inch | 1.2 | cm |
| 3/4 | inch | 2 | cm |
| 1 | inch | 2.5 | cm |
| 1 1/4 | inches | 3.1 | cm |
| 1 1/2 | inches | 3.7 | cm |
| 2 | inches | 5 | cm |
| 3 | inches | 7.5 | cm |
| 4 | inches | 10 | cm |
| 5 | inches | 12.5 | cm |

## APPROXIMATE EQUIVALENTS

1 kilo is slightly more than 2 pounds

1 liter is slightly more than 1 quart

1 meter is slightly more than 3 feet

1 centimeter is approximately 3/4 inch